48 Rules of Power
The Power of Your Mind

By Commissioner George Mentz JD MBA CWM

Contents

First published by
Mentzinger Media, LTD

http://www.gmentz.com
Endorsed by the Academy http://www.gafm.com

© George Mentz 2020
The right of George Mentz to be identified as the author of this work has been asserted in accordance with the Copyright, Designs and Patents Act 1988.
ISBN – Disclosed on Publishing
ISBN - Disclosed on Publishing

Library of Congress Cataloguing-in-Publication Data
Cataloguing in Publication Data

A catalogue record for this book is available online

Preface

If you have read empowerment and self-help books, many of these books are quite similar in nature, and these success books talk about dealing with people, leading, managing, money, making good decisions, building things, cultivating the type of attitude that is necessary to have for success.

So, there are a lot of common themes in self-help books. But, if you read a top Success Book, each is a little bit different. Some books are a bit more straight forward, they have a more WEALTH consciousness ideas built into them. This type of book is a no-nonsense, honest, and straight forward approach that doesn't want to waste anyone's time, but just wants to give you the facts and the information needed to get the job done.

How the Mind Creates Your World—The Path to Abundance

The definition of abundance and true wealth is arguably the free and unrestricted use of all the things that may be necessary for you to advance in the direction of your dreams and potential, thus attaining your fullest mental, spiritual, and physical prosperity. You have a right to wealth. Wealth is that basic desire to have a richer, fuller, and more abundant life. We all should live for the equal advancement and fulfillment of body, mind, and soul; there is no reason we should limit our capacities in any of the three sectors.

Many associate greed, lust, and arrogance as a constituent of the rich, and they wonder if wealthy people are truly happy. Ironically, it is poverty which disheartens the spirit in human relationships, including those we love. Poverty undermines self-esteem, confidence, and our outlook upon life. With poverty as a state of mind and life, we are empty to give to those whom we love and care about. Poverty limits our ability to connect to people and the world. Poverty incapacitates giving, which is the demonstration of love and compassion.

Abundance and creation are forms of wealth, and therefore we must get in tune with creativity. When we do, prosperity will appear in our lives.

Creativity, innovation, and abundance will go to the people who flow and cooperate with life and not reject it. Nature has an inexhaustible source of riches. Accordingly, it is natural to seek more from life, and your advancement is vital for your growth. As the saying goes, we grow or die. With a higher plane and dimension, we can now make forty years' worth of advancement in three to six years, with efficiency.

As an example, the last one hundred years of science have shown more life-giving and technological improvements than the last two thousand years. This is proof that rapid advancement is available with freedom and discipline at your command.

We will now show you the first secret of life. This key to success can be yours if you simply accept the following statement. Just take it as fact, and the world will begin to move with you.

Thoughts and Wealth Creation

How we construct our thoughts and emotions assists in the manifestation of physical forms and our character. Our worldview is also malleable and can be a great catalyst to creation. Positive and negative thinking facilitates constructive or deconstructive results. For instance, the statement "I need more money" lends the subject to continual detrimental thoughts to "need more money." Changing the focus to a goal (having more money) rather than the problem (needing more money) results in a positive perspective. Rephrasing this thought in a positive manner would be, "I will find opportunity that yields greater and greater rewards."

If you conceive of your desire, you can then imagine that your goal will take place with belief, and then, you will be able retrieve the opportunity from the world's storehouse of riches. As a rule, man originates thought; thought turns into plans or mental images in the mind. Man can communicate his thought and mental images into and throughout the world. This creation begins with our thoughts focused within and without. Your mind is the center of your world. Your thoughts, mixed with a thankful heart directed toward your goals, can flow out into the world as creative energy. You mentally picture and believe that your healthy goal is possible. Understand the essence and reasons that you should have this type of result in your life; you envision your desired outcome with specificity. You think of and picture the opportunity frequently, and you believe that you have the type of result that you desire, feeling it and harvesting the emotion of having it as much as possible.

These thoughts and a mental practice of visualization will be sent off into the world like a letter of request. If you practice this visualization enough, the desires you have will be met. Truth is your faithful, non-doubting interpretation of your thoughts. Do not focus on failure, poverty, disease, or deficiencies—your truth is health, riches, success, and happiness. Do not doubt or speak against your thoughts and dreams. Keep these mental petitions as faithful as possible while living harmoniously with people, places, institutions, and the universe.

It is the desire of the Source that you should have all that you need. You will begin with a simple desire for some type of improvement in life; a desire coupled with unwavering faith will correctly unfold for you over time. The motives of your desires are important: you want to help yourself and others, and you do not want to cause harm in the process.

You will achieve these desires much more quickly if your motives are not colored with greed, ego, pride, lust, competition, hate, resentment, and arrogance. Your desires must be propelled by love, gratitude, faith, confidence, mental focus, truth, acceptance, creativity, positive expectation, and clear planning, and you should give more love and value than you take.

Desire and Purpose

Desire is the motivating force that rules the world. Even with today's attitudes—where science, philosophy, and religious metaphysics cross paths—most have acknowledged that: finding purpose, natural expression, mission, and one's true place are all major factors in self-expression and spirit-manifestation. Where a person's true purpose is frustrated, reactions take place, and most people are guided and again redirected by their burning desires toward their highest ideal of creativity and function.

To Begin Your Process of Prosperity

Brainstorm on your ideas each day, clarifying in your mind exactly what you want and how you will achieve it. Hold the picture of the moment you have completed the achievement with positive certainty; never speak or think of it as not being possible, and claim the picture of success as a fact and that it is already yours in mind. Keep your mind tuned in to the universal presence and energy by having a thankful heart and grateful thoughts. If you cannot be grateful, then begin to think of your ability to walk, talk, see, hear, travel, and speak. These are the simplest of freedoms to be grateful for, and they are easily overlooked. Good health is one of these simple freedoms we should recognize with gratitude; in doing so, it initiates a powerful, positive outlook. This new perspective connects you to life and your dreams. People will soon sense this new outlook and serenity that you are projecting.

Remember that you must exercise this mental picturing and thankfulness every day for at least a month. However, after a month, you will not believe the difference in your perception of life. Do not be frightened or ashamed to ask for what you really want. Ask for more than you need. The world is full of people to give and receive. Never be frightened to receive—receive with humility, thankfulness, and appreciation. In the final analysis, extreme poverty and self-sacrifice are not pleasing to anyone, and extreme altruism is just as dangerous as extreme greed. Thus, give and receive with joy.

There is a creative universal force from which unlimited abundance flows. It will give us all that we need and desire when we have a pure heart. A pure heart and mind simply means that you do not allow the weeds of ignorance, bitterness, hate, and irritation to cloud and fill your mind. To facilitate a mind of purity, make the profound connection to the universal spirit within by developing a strong feeling of thankfulness for life, love, health, and material gifts that you already have or will have.

Let us think about gratitude and thankfulness. Can you have happiness with a bitter heart? Can you have real faith when you are constantly blaming, angry, and ungrateful? If you think you can be happy with a blaming, hateful, and bitter mind, then good luck. If you want to change to an outlook on life where you feel that all is possible, then keep reading.

Think back and reflect on the times in your life when you got what you wanted and became arrogant or egotistical. After you received some good fortune, you forgot your humility and abandoned your connection to your universal Spirit. You may have given up your relationship with spirituality because you thought you had won the game of life.

In times of good fortune, it is especially important to exercise and practice grateful thoughts. Doing so continues the flow of riches to us and expands your focus. What becomes important to you will come to you and remain with you. If you have doubt and fear, you will disperse fear and doubt. Gratitude will keep you connected to the world and afford you a harmonious relationship with all, because gratitude and thankfulness prevent dissatisfaction. Continue to fix your attention in appreciation for the best in life; fix your mind on health, love, success, and good fortune. Your faith will be renewed and strengthened from your own consciousness of gratitude.

Energize Gratitude

There are many ways to promote greater peace of mind. Generally, there is no better method to increase a sense of tranquility than to cultivate a mindset of thankfulness. A good mental practice is to add a five-minute gratitude exercise to your daily routine.   Think about or write out a list of things for which to be grateful for today. This exercise will brings wondrous results. You may not feel results overnight, but within a month you will feel and see the change toward a positive perspective, which becomes a greater worldview. In addition to gratitude, exercise a ban on negativity for one week. Complaining attracts destructive people, places, and things into your life. Each time you find yourself complaining, touch each of your shoulders with your finger and proclaim, "I am abundance."

If you have trouble with certain negative triggers, then eliminate them. If politics bothers you, then quit reading the paper for a short while. If certain people constantly annoy you, then you should avoid them for a time, too. You are working on yourself, and it is okay to take care of your well-being first. The people around you will be happy in the end, if you rebuild and renew your positive spirit and enthusiasm for life as a priority. This is putting your health first, in this case your spiritual health.

Success Agreement

Your desires should be very specific, and your mental blueprint must be just as precise. For example, you may write out on a piece of paper a personal agreement with yourself:

I, Jane Doe, will have a successful business and I will live in a beautiful three-thousand-square-foot home in the Tudor style near Central Park. I am the best I can be in my job and company, and I am very successful in my position, selling creative products and services. I give the highest quality service and value to my clients. My products and services will have outstanding benefits and will help all of my customers. I do all of these things, work hard, and be persistent in my purpose and labor. I will not give up. People will be glad to pay me for my services because they are a benefit to all. I gladly accept compensation and do what I need to do to receive the payment. I will use the fruits of my creativity to build my business, invest in myself, enjoy life, help those I love, follow my dreams, and live in the home of my dreams.

Send Your Petition to the World like a Rrequest That Must Be Granted

Spend each day contemplating your personal commitment. Visualize the success and form an attractive mental image—moving into your beautiful home, helping those you love, or a bonus check for great work. Mentally imagine yourself in that very moment of completing the transaction with joy. Feel it, gather the emotion, and believe that an outcome (or an even better one) is possible. Moreover, you should know, feel, and see in your mind what you will do when you have the wonderful home or outstanding wealth. Then think how you will live, help others, and serve humanity.

A clearer picture strengthens our desire. If your desire is strong, your willingness to focus on the success and to claim it as yours will become a seamless transaction. Each day you must engage your heartfelt faith to secure small steps toward success. Stay engaged in moving ahead with your goals amid gratitude and faith. After you picture your optimal vision and read your personal agreement to yourself, complete the meditative thought process with words of gratitude: "Thank you for the blessing," "Thank you for expanding the quality of my life," and "Thank you for protecting me and my family." This will complete your exercise. Send this petition into the world like a request that must be granted. Then, you should be ready to receive what you want in any form, or even a higher result.

As for willpower, you need only cultivate the idea of willingness upon yourself. Your self-will should be used to think about precise constructive plans and doing specific beneficial actions. Every moment spent in uncertainty is a waste of time—direct your attention to prosperity. The best thing you can do for the non-believers is to show them that you can achieve abundance and success. Your efforts will be a success if your actions are based in a strong desire where you are willing to go the distance to fulfill it.

Do not tell the same doubtful people of your dreams and ideas. If you tell enough bitter people about your idea, their collective doubt or jealousy may weaken and sabotage your energy. Surround yourself with successful people, experts in the field, and people who are encouraging and insightful and working toward a new outlook on life.

Always See the Positive Side of Your Present State of Affairs

Interest yourself in becoming rich in life, and always try to see the positive side of your present state of affairs. Focus on optimistic conversation or beneficial events that have happened in your life. Make lists of things to do and begin doing them one by one. It may take a year to complete, but you must begin somewhere. Do each series of tasks and individual actions efficiently. Don't worry about the past or the future or incessantly moan to others about your difficulties or failures. Focus on prosperity today.

Do Only What Can Be Done Today

Take action today. Write our plans for your future for this year, the next 3 years, and even 5 or 10 years in the future. Begin to do tasks each day to improve your lot in life and help others.   Do your tasks correctly the first time, and you need not fix them later. To do efficient and effective work, you need only to do one thing at a time and to not spread yourself too thin. Focus on the now and make your plans incremental or step-driven. One step at a time, with focus and effectiveness, will virtually guarantee success.

You need not try and mandate an outcome. The creative forces will unfold the correct and highest result for you; you merely need to aim in the direction of your dreams with focus and organize your affairs, so that you are prepared to receive the success and gladly accept the payoff. Overall, action is what will allow you to receive your abundance. Do only what can be done today, and tomorrow you can begin anew. In sum, put the faith, vision, and purpose behind your every action to accelerate the path to your higher abundance.

Find Out What You Really Want to Do and Be! - Write a List of Twenty Things of Interest to You Life's Purpose

You should determine what you like and what you love to do through this simple process. Write a list of twenty things of interest to you; continue adding and subtracting from the list. Over time, you will development meaningful ideas because your higher consciousness will guide you toward your given talents. As a note, your purpose could be to research history or science, to read books, to write articles or books, to develop written content, to draw or create art and graphics, to travel, or to communicate with people. Over time your definite purpose should become more specific, such as "I intend to become the best speaker or writer on the topic of politics or taxes, complete a masters or doctorate in international business, and build the best website for information and links to success literature." It does not matter how you start, just begin the writing process! Remember that a good talent (something you like to do and you are good at doing) combined with desire to become the best in a given field of work will ensure that you will do what you love. At the least, you can become a trainer of your trade or profession and give back to the world by accelerating the learning of children or students in your field.

Without being boastful, you must convey the impression to others that you are an exemplarily human being for all who come in contact with you. Impress on others that you can add to their lives; speak of your life and business as getting better and better all of the time. Act and feel as though you are successful, as if you are already rich in life and all your needs are met. Incorporate a compassionate humility that you blend with poise, faith, confidence, and self-esteem. You need only speak when necessary, but your strong character and faithful confidence will attract the best people into your life.

Use Your Present Job Skillfully to Move in the Direction That You Want

If you are in a job and cannot leave it to immediately follow your dreams, then do what you can in the evenings or weekends to hone your skills, plans, and education toward your goal. Use your existing position to move in the direction that you want. There are thousands of people who have their business pay for their part-time education; your contacts at work may even lead to a better or different job. In business, you must also be prepared to discuss your dreams (what you want from life) in spoken words. You should know exactly what you want, and you should be able to clarify and quantify your ideas to others in an enthusiastic way. Be able to ask for and accept what you want out of life. You will need to interact with others who can help you. This process of abundance, harmonization, and advancement will lead others to want to help you. Be ready for them, and be open to forming alliances with others. Thus, your visions, meditations, and requests are traditionally answered by the universal power in the form of other people or entities being available to help and guide you—be ready to tell them what you need. Do not be ashamed to ask for win-win relationships with the people that come to you.

Times Are about as Good as You Allow Them to Become

In conclusion, times are only as good as your mind perceives them. Just when you think you are failing is the exact moment to continue your gratitude, meditating on your goals and action! That moment of doubt is when the highest good for you is ready to unfold; sometimes people call this grace. Even if the result is not exactly as you want, something better is coming to you at the right time and place. Therefore, you are many times protected from a bad outcome or relationship by waiting a little longer and preparing yourself for a better situation.

Our Thoughts, Actions, Inactions, and Omissions Create Our Character

Overall, repeated thoughts become tendencies or habits, willingness and willpower can initiate action, and repeated experiences lead to wisdom. Our combined thoughts, actions, inactions, and omissions are what create the totality of our character.

If we desire prosperous and peaceful energy, we must be willing to put out good thoughts, praise others, become thankful, see things in an opportunistic light, and have faith in the regeneration of mind and body. Our every action and thought of goodness is very powerful. Acts of kindness, service to others, and self-development are all extremely powerful energies. Negative feelings are feeble thoughts that are a hundred times less powerful than acts of creation and constructiveness. If we maintain a harmonious relationship with others while keeping a peaceful relationship with ourselves, then life can be much easier. Further, when we are avoiding wasteful thinking and actions, our spiritual energies may maintain their laser focus and power. As with physics, it is possible to neutralize a sound wave by setting up another sound wave of the same pattern that comes from the opposite pole. Therefore it is possible to conjure and visualize ideas, thoughts, and images that can completely neutralize old attitudes. By changing your outlook, you can change your future. Every cause has its effect, and every action has its results, but it is desire that is the link that connects the two. Thinking on a higher level requires a mind that is free, lean, efficient, harmonious, and clear. Gratitude and attunement will afford us the clarity to absorb prosperity and build anew/

The Psychology of Bio-Hacking - 12 Step Cheat Sheet to Abundance
How to Write Your Own Horoscopes of Success
By: Commissioner George Mentz, JD MBA CILS – Counselor of Laws

At any age, people may need to reboot their lives. Some need to start over completely while others may need a new start or a leg up in life. These ideas are critical to those who want advanced growth in their life. If you are familiar with success events, cognitive therapy, boot camps, or 12-step work, you know that in 6 months to a year, a person's life can fundamentally change and be redirected toward usefulness, a higher purpose, or a destiny of their calling.

Here are 12 individual "Bio Hacking" [i] steps to innovation, success, health, wealth, and prosperity. These steps are a framework for radical advancement of your life, mindset, performance, and success. Read these concepts carefully, using a dictionary if you must. Each sentence within each step may be the most important concept that you have ever read. Some ideas may seem trivial when compared to the major issues going on in your life; however, the steps are for a broad audience looking for growth and advancement.

After you have read this, read it again and underline your favorite points. Think about the key strategies herein. While much of the information presented here is perennial wisdom, some of the teachings in this short essay may be new, bold, powerful, and daunting. I urge you to read the whole essay several times to ensure that it sinks in. After that, you may be able to implement some of the greatest enhancements of your life in just a matter of weeks.

Here are the 12 steps of abundance and wholeness in short form.

1. **Beliefs, Clearing, and Programming** - What do you want from life? What are solutions to your problems? Refine your beliefs;

clear out what isn't working; reinvent yourself for peak wholeness, happiness, and effectiveness in life.

2. **Renew Mind** – Refining & Defining the MINDSET – Seek inspiration and ideas, write goals, define tasks. Learn to make great choices after clearing and preparing for a new goal or new life, you must renew and fill you mind and body with constructive and empowering information, ideas, goals, and beliefs.

3. **Declare Your Aims -** Evaluate yourself, augment your senses, and affirm what you want.

4. **Learn how to Charge Your Brain** – Begin to mentally change your fate and fortune through thankfulness and mindful action.

5. **Empowering Yourself** – Esoteric growth is a process of developing self regard and your inner powers. Learn self love, learn to love life and others though the secrets of these steps.

6. **Purpose & Viewpoint** – Manifest a constructive worldview - A mindful worldview changes experience AND experience changes your consciousness. Being mindful and introspective while in action is the key to efficiency and effectiveness.

7. **Harmoniousness** – Be in love with your soul and with your spirituality within. Radiate zeal and find a positive connection to your world.

8. **Decree and Comprehend** – Speak of what you want in your mind and out loud. Prepare for success and learn about what you want.

9. **Aliveness** - Live well and enjoy your life – Learning to plan, act, survive, excel, live, love, and enjoy. Learning what you love to do while learning to enjoy your success. Learn how to enjoy your success and serenity and learn to invest in yourself for the benefit of all concerned.

10.   **Acceptance** - Refuse to accept struggle and lack. Demand improvement and incremental success in your life and your mindset.

11.   **Wisdom** – Every idea or goal may require you to acquire knowledge or experience. Find out what you need to know to accomplish your goals. Cultivate your mind, body, and spirit to maximize your potential for yourself and those you love.

12.   **Action** – Why not start it today? Go and *get* it. Go and *be* it. Go and *have* it. Take ownership and responsibility for your destiny. Continue to evaluate and monitor your successes and goals while being a serene warrior of excellence.

Perhaps you are seeking a solution to a situation, wanting innovation and improvement, or you are seeking greater expression in various areas of your life including relationships, health, love, work, and play. The goal is to take your mind to the next level. Remember, just a 2-3% improvement of your cognitive and mental abilities above normal would provide you with almost super human performance. The key to using these steps is to learn to live above struggle; existing in a higher order of joy, success, aliveness, and purposeful living.

Here are the Steps in Long Form with Expanded Descriptions

1. **Beliefs, Clearing, and Programming** - Develop a strident belief that the Universe wants the best for you at all times and will provide for you at all times if you cooperate with the immutable laws of achievement. **Purify – Learn to Diagnose Problems, Identify Opportunities, Empty Problems and Fill with Desire, Objectives, and Potential.** Become ready and willing to write your own horoscope and program your own mind with the destiny you seek. Release and repudiate petty external forces that affect your dominant thought patterns and ability to reach your potential. **Decide what is true.** Determine what ideas to accept as true. Use the ideas that work best to be pragmatic. If

you are lacking in health and prosperity, you may have a subconscious mindset of unworthiness, shame, scarcity, and frustration or feelings of anger. **Rewrite Your Drive** - These old ideas can be overwritten, they can be dissipated with effort, using emptying and filling strategies. **Reject Bullshit** - You must deny and reject what you don't what in your life and purge old non-constructive ideas.

2. **Renew Mind** – Refining and defining the MINDSET into the consciousness that you seek. Do what you need to do to purge the ideas and thoughts that do not serve your happiness and success. Clear your mindset for a new and improved set of beliefs and objectives. When your mental and spiritual hard drive is clear, it becomes ready for a new set of programs and performance. **Choice** - Our greatest power is the power of choice and action. We can be discerning in what we bring into our mind, lives, and hearts. There is power in bold thinking and actions. **Writing goals** down helps you impress the objectives on your mind and stay a few chess moves ahead which opens up opportunities and ideas. Always write out what you want, putting pen to paper clarifies and distills your focus and purpose. Write out the **incremental steps** you need to take to achieve your goals. If you write or type them, put them where you can see them every day. Nobody knows you better than yourself. If you can tune into your higher self, you can illuminate and discover your authentic purpose and desires. **Flow of Ideas** - If you can get into a meditative place and relax, you can allow the inspiration of the universe or the ideas of the universe to come to you. You can act on this higher will by analyzing those ideas. If the ideas are honest, mindful, unselfish, and loving, you will find great power in these ideas.

3. **Declare Your Aims** – Choosing what you want to be, do, and have. At some point, we must pick what we will do with our time and ability and focus our desires on what we want to do

and where we want to go. Think beyond what you have been told you can do or achieve, **question YOURSELF.** What else am I missing or truly seeking to be, do, or have? **Affirmations** help re-write your neuron connections and DNA. Leaving new imprints on your mind of the reasonableness of success is important. Learning to believe that success and happiness is a reasonable option can transform your life's direction for the better. Try mental affirmation, visual, verbal auto suggestion (repetition of positive statements), notes, signs, symbols, charms, poetry, music, video, trance, and dance. **Visualize** what you want to be, do, and have. Release the mental masterpiece of your "completed goals" into the world and allow the universe to work on it for you at night while you sleep. **Augment the Senses** - The next day, practice imagining the life you aspire to achieve to see, feel while practicing having the results in your deeper mind with emotion and sensation.

4. **Charge Your Brain** – Charging your purpose and belief with intent and emotions such as love and aliveness. When we take command of our thoughts and emotions, we can take control of the direction of our life. **Hacking Fortune and Fate** – In ancient Europe, there are myths of fate or the three maidens of fortune. In Rome they called them the Fortuna, in Scandinavia, they were called the Three Norns or Fates. They were said to weave the future. There is the maiden of the past, maiden of the present, and maiden of the future or what will be. It is important to weave your own future by contributing energy and mindful acts to the now to create a pattern of the past which combined with actions and thinking of today, manifests future of possibilities.

Thankfulness - After researching human performance for decades, it is also critical to integrate a worldview of opportunity and possibility. This can be done by incorporating gratitude and thankfulness into your daily life. Gratitude is an ingredient of peace of mind and love. Such a powerful ingredient can allow your mind and brain to function at a higher level of clarity. Rather than incessantly focusing on what is wrong, if we can refocus on what is good and right with our home, relationships, and life; then, we can cultivate a mindset of contentment, prosperity, and abundance. Gratitude has a special power to keep us in harmonious relationship with the spirit and laws of the universe. It is important to purge your mind, letting go of the dead weight of resentments, anger, unworthiness, or even hatred. With this clearing work, we can then learn to fill our minds with powerful and constructive thoughts of courage, patience, kindness, love, peace, humility, love, and generosity. Accordingly, the best way to charge the brain with productive dominant thoughts is to dedicate your thinking toward a dominant mindset of positivity and harmony.

5. **Empower Yourself** – Respect yourself and your inner esoteric power. Learning to understand and respect the immutable laws of the universe, will allow you to work in harmony with the elements. **Harmoniousness** - Master harmony with self and with others. A harmonious mindset attracts and deserves wealth and health because it is open to good and vibrates in a way that does not repel abundance. Remember that if you are always vibrating about negative thoughts, jealousy, envy, or resentment, your inherent state of being may repel your opportunities. However, if your mindset is one of enthusiasm, worthiness, aspiration, harmony and success, then you would be mentally more award of opportunities and have a clear ability to respond. **Worthiness** – You must decide, internalize, and act as if you are worthy of life's blessings. What is your self image and dominant conception of your self-image? You only receive what you subconsciously allow yourself to have. The better you treat yourself; the better quality of people you will have in your life. Education, skills, appearances, etc. cultivate a

harmonious positive relationship with health, self, love, and wealth. Master body, mind, and spirit through exercise you enjoy, a healthy diet, periodic fellowship, and healthy REM sleep. With this balance you can also boost your mind by learning new skills and tactically enhancing your performance toward your goals. Become connected with the powers of the universe rather than disconnected.

6. **Purpose & Viewpoint** – A mindful worldview changes experience and experience changes consciousness. Being mindful and introspective while in action is the key to efficiency and effectiveness. **Unambiguousness** - Be definite about what you want and know how to ask for it. Know how to illuminate your "elevator pitch" of goals to your mind and god. **Articulate Mental Energy into the Universe** - You may need to affirm and decree in prayer and aloud the things that you want to best imprint the objectives into your deeper mind. Model yourself after the tactics of great leaders and winners but find your own style and authenticity. It is said that one of the only ways to increase efficiency of a worker already using proven strategies of success is to allow them to have and master their own style. **UC=UB=UR** – What you dominantly see yourself as being in your mind is what you become, what you become is what and who you are….

7. **Love** – Be in love with your soul and with your inner spirituality. Self love is extremely powerful and manifests as charisma and enthusiasm. Controlling your charisma can make you into a powerful relationship builder whether in business, private life, or business negotiations. **Radiate Zeal** - Love your inner higher self, love what you desire, love what you seek, and what you need. When you love yourself, you will love others. When you allow yourself to love others, you will love yourself better. **Connectedness** - Your harmonious connection to the universe is the foundation of your power and awareness and possessing

clarity of mind is like having a computer that is not overloaded with junk and is virus free. Remember, most people believe that the spark of creation is within themselves. Learn to love and value that spark that connects you to the vast energy of the universe.

8. **Decree** – Speak of what you want in your mind and out loud. A decree can be verbal, mental, prayerful, mindful, written, or put down into the form of a sign, symbol, musical composition, poem, charm/sigil, video, or dance. Use these forms of incantations and written commands to program your mind and beliefs to achieve peak potential. Make sure happiness, love, success, and financial freedom matter to you. **Impress Your Mind** - How will you continue to impress the life you want and deserve upon your subconscious mind? You can use specific goal selection, tactical training, imagination, visualization, auto-suggestion, brain training, self talk, affirmations, notes to yourself, mapping, treasure maps, and more.

9. **Aliveness** - Live Well – Learn to plan, act, survive, excel, live, love, and enjoy. Learning what you love to do while learning to enjoy your success. Allow yourself the relationships, assets, and opportunities you deserve. **Prepare the table** – Prepare for what you seek, keeping in mind that you must be able to receive your good. Prepare your mind, body, appearance, skills, etc. **Comprehension** - You must comprehend what you want (who, what when, and how) of what you seek to be, do, or have. You must learn to have the success in your mind's eye, have your mind know how to accomplish it, know and be the success before it happens, to accomplish your goals.

10.   **Acceptance** - Refuse to accept struggle. Demand improvement and incremental success in your life and your

mindset. Break out to accept new greatness of your life. ACCEPT YOUR GOOD and LET GO of NEGATIVE THINKING. Be a champion and ditch the blaming and complaining. **Remain Tuned in to Opportunities** - Keep your conscious mind tuned in/aware of the good we desire and deserve. You want a good life with the freedom to work and travel when and where you want. Maintain intense awareness of your acts, words, and deeds. **Maintain Receptiveness** - Make clear to your mind what you want. Speak to your mind and send images of success to it at receptive moments of the day. Keep your primary purpose at the forefront of your heart, mind, and subconscious.

11.   **Wisdom** – Every idea or goal may require you to acquire knowledge. Find out what you need to know to accomplish your goals. Cultivate your mind, body and spirit in order to maximize your potential for yourself and those you love. **Find Joy** - Scan your memory for occasions which gave you joy. What was in those moments? Was it travel, people, winning, achieving peace that you felt while using your skills? What energizes you? Find your labor of love, your calling, and you will serve humanity, enjoy wholeness, and achieve success. Align with those who you are supposed to be in this period of life. Alignment and wisdom work with each other to give you peace, power, and poise. Wisdom comes from the universe. Stay tuned into it; maintain clarity of mind; seek inspiration; and act on great ideas.

12.   **Action** – Why not start reaching your goals today? Go and get it. Go and be it. Go and have it. Take ownership of and responsibility for your destiny. Seize upon two or three things to do each day toward your optimum health, happiness, success, and relationships. Take a moment to praise yourself for something you did well today. Praise somebody else for doing

something with excellence. Taking command of assets and money. Making assets and money serve you. Use your money wisely to invest in body mind and soul growth, your loved ones, and invest in your opportunities. **Self Motivation** is critical. We must trick our minds into continuous improvement of doing, acting, making phone calls, emailing, marketing, closing, working out, preparing, and performing. **Pragmatism** - Exceptional dedication, imagination, practice, and preparation equals exceptional results. **DO IT** - Don't worry about the WHY, do what works.

The best way to begin these steps is to take a hard look at your track record for the last 1-5 years. Were the last few years a good period in your life? Can you do better? Do you want more? As a law professor, I would say that you either have a good case or a bad one. You either have the law on your side or not. You either have quality evidence to support your claim or you don't. You can either win or lose. In law, if you prove your case by a preponderance of the evidence, that is just a level of proof that is greater than 50%. Life can be the same. If you are operating at a level of 49% or less, you are losing at the game of life each day. If you can improve by just more than 1+%, you are now considered a winner in the metaphysical court of law. It is just that simple! Once you believe that you are happy, healthy and prosperous 51% or more of the time; then, you are above water and you may continuously feel like you have super human abilities in contract to before.

When discussing the greatest philosophers and psychologists, it is hard to miss their emphasis on human potential and human performance. Top thinkers of the past put a focus on character, thinking, habits, and skills, but they also focus on the use of the consciousness. The great Ralph Waldo Emerson suggested in his writings that fortune is the fruit of your character; and the great Descartes mused over how mankind is equipped to rule over nature and be creative in a way that expresses excellence. From the stoics to Jeremy Bentham stated that minimizing struggle is a key objective in maximizing pleasure and success.

If you are familiar with the Danish Philosopher Soren Kierkegaard, his writings demonstrate that life can be viewed as a task based on the free, responsible choices of individuals which is an existentialist viewpoint. As individuals, Kierkegaard suggested that seekers should detach themselves from the herd mentality, and discover their own world view and nurture their own unique meaning for life. However, our world view is subject to many key variables. If we learn to manipulate the variables and cooperate with the principles of nature, we can achieve a greater self actualization. Self actualization is the degree to which an individual's predispositions are expressed in talents and work. [ii] The prime determinants of professional behavior are to be found in the need for love, esteem, and self expression and self-actualization. [iii]

According to Schopenhauer, the phenomenal world is not so chaotic but rather operates according to sufficient reason or a set of guidelines. Schopenhauer implies that the immutable laws of the universe operate with causality or "cause and effect.' Schopenhauer also sees willpower as a kind of force that is always seeking higher expression that strives to not only survive but to grow.

Dr. Victor Frankl espoused that life always has meaning even if that meaning or purpose is not clear at the time. Frankl believed that each person comes into life with unique potentialities to fulfill. To make it more personal, my father, Judge/Sgt. Henry Mentz, believed that his purpose or meaning for his platoon in 1945 was to win the war in Europe, liberate the people, and free the starving prison camp survivors such as Dr. Victor Frankl.

Dr. William James, the father of modern psychology believed that if we can minimize the gap between our potential and our self actualization, we will have a higher self-regard. Similarly, Carl Jung, who is the godfather of "Analytical Psychology" believed that

Individuation is becoming what you always were meant to be [**potentia** (Latin)] where you fulfill your unique purpose. Dr. Jung famously said, "*Spiritus contra spiritum*" which literally translates to "spirit against spirit." Loosely translated, it refers to "a spiritual experience is the only way to counter a deadly affliction of the spirit such as addiction.

As with Spinoza, Einstein believed that the universe is governed by impersonal natural laws where Einstein actually said, "I believe in Spinoza's God." Einstein probably meant that there is substance in all things that may be unseen such as in quantum physics, but if you realize how to cooperate with the impersonal laws of your environment, you can and will prosper at a higher level than others but that does not mean perfection or the elimination of the glitches in the scatter chart of probabilities.

There are various laws that we take for granted such as the laws of electricity, thermodynamics, aerodynamics, principle of least resistance, and so forth. For example, the path of least resistance is the physical or metaphorical pathway that provides the least resistance to forward motion by a given object or entity, among a set of alternative paths. With the use of the mind and action, there are various ways to cooperate, engage, or avoid people places and things. To engage learning, to avoid dangerous situations, to maximize strength in body, mind and spirit are all ways to lead a more efficient and effective lifestyle. However, you can do many things right, but if you still do "one thing" incessantly destructive, you can blow up your life regardless of your good traits. I have seen celebrities, rock stars, royalty, and millionaires lose everything to drugs and addictions while also going to the gym, doing yoga and attending church each week. So, the moral of the story is to maximize constructive behavior and stay clear of destructive things. Get a plan and use methods and activities to expand your life, love, and friendships.

If you can dig deep and change yourself from the inside out, and begin to use great habits on a daily basis, you begin to stack the cosmic cards of life in your favor and you win at life's celestial casino going forward. Famous sales gurus often say that the difference between failure and great success can be as little as 2% more effort each day than other folks. Thus, we must all learn to control our dominant thoughts and habits while rejecting and avoiding needless scarcity and struggle based thinking. All pessimists have is their opinion of failure and "they are determined to be right about what is wrong with this world."

As they say, belief is the acceptance of something as truth. Once you accept a belief, that acceptance begins to create new realities for you and you begin to experience life in a whole new way.

In conclusion, there are no poor people but rather only those who are determined to struggle without advancement. Wealth can be defined as the state of being rich in life including possessing the material prosperity to meet your needs. Wealth is also relative health, wholeness, personal success, and a general feeling of prosperity. Learn to rely more on your higher self, your inner consciousness, and your 6th sense. If you are working these steps, you will have more ideas, more creativity, and more persistence to go after what you seek to expand your life. Life, in general, will meet you in the way that you reach out and greet life and seek life. We may all reap what we sow, but this requires us to take present day action each day, plant the seeds of ideas, give our all, and manifest successful tasks and goals one-by-one.

Affirmation Statements to Maximize Your Creative Power

The purpose of these ideas is to open your mind to the impersonal, benign and abundant powers of the universe and its energy on a quantum level. Read each idea and let it soak in. If you disagree with an idea, go to the next one. Try and cultivate a belief in the steps that work for you.

1. We must come to believe that our mental energy and the energy of the universe are similar and that both cooperate with and affect each other on a quantum level..

2. This potential similarity or oneness between the individual and the impersonal laws of the cosmos, when claimed and unified to a degree of quality, allows the practitioner to make intentional impressions of desire upon the framework of the universe to manifest life, objects, events, and opportunity.

3. Thoughts are energy and also things. "We think, therefore, life is". Build your character and self-regard that is conducive to your desires through the use of positive words, ideas and deeds.

4. Harmony, gratitude, and clarity of mind allow for the efficient transference of desire upon the creative mind and universal spirit.

5. We expand and innovate our beliefs by allowing constructive ideas and attitudes into our conscious and subconscious mind so as to hold new patterns of higher thought.

6. Your vital energy is our financial abundance. Both physical energy and mental energy. Energy combined with the catalyst of relative faith or belief can be more powerful in creating desired circumstances or objectives.

7. We interpret, create and apply the meaning to events, people, places and things. Thus our mental interpretive vibration affects

our: desires, results and events and even our memory of the events.

8. We have the ability to construct, deconstruct, and arrange the information that is received and perceived by our senses. We have the ability to construct, deconstruct, and arrange our dominant thoughts, desires and intentions. This ability helps us use our imaginative, planning and emotional mind.

9. Set Intentions Well. Make sure you aim or plan is in writing where you have itemized generally, what you need to think and do to allow the intention to be brought into this world.

10.   To cooperate efficiently with the universal law, do something that makes you feel alive, that empowers you, that allows enthusiasm. Determine the purpose of your chief aim and how your goals will help improve the lives of others with solutions and value.

11.   We must learn to direct our dominant thoughts. We cannot be a mental and spiritual house divided. Our mind must be focused upon the potentiality or possibility of our desire occurring in our favor. The more focused we are on the good chances of your desire occurring, the better. The key is to hold this dominant focus above 50% in the direction of our ideals.

12.   Impassion your desires and thoughts upon your end goal. Energize your ideas and intentions with constructive enthusiasm and heartfelt thanks for the success coming our way.

13.   Take effective actions each day & all day toward any task that helps fulfill your dreams. Organize tasks that concentrate and focus energy toward success and prioritize you're your life around larger goals and momentum toward your objectives.

14.   Insulate your mind with peace, harmony, gratitude; belief had "positive humility". Humility means that you are teachable, and have the ability to adapt and innovate at any time. Do this

while seeking conscious connection with the Spirit of the Universe.

15.   Avoid people, places and things that stand to block or inhibit you from happiness, achievement, and health.

16.   Seed things to happen each day with actions, deeds, outreach, public relations, branding etc. Use this seeding process and then allow for the receipt of rewards from this seeding. Make sure you have the ability to receive and act upon the rewards.

17.   Build self regard and confidence. Get the mind, body, look, skills and connections that you need to become who you want. Become the person who has what you want on the INSIDE.

18.   Maintain your vibration and connection to the Spiritual Energy of the Universe on a daily basis. If you feel out of sorts or ineffective, take time to reconnect, settle down, and focus with thanks.

19.   Speak and think dominant streams of constructive thoughts. Practice this exercise like a meditation if you can.

20.   Remain care free with an open heart. Be open to new ideas and success.

21.   Do not be desperate, if the people you want to work with don't need you, find somebody else who does.

22.   Align your beliefs with your dreams. Get past the fear of getting into the new life or new project.

23.   Be knowledgeable about what you want, and be able to verbally explain it.

24.   Be willing to commit 100% to your aim. Your willingness and enthusiasm for your idea or goal will fuel your persistence and power.

25.   Understand that engaging work and tasks actually creates ideas, builds a vibration, attracts opportunity.

26.   Remember, if you can't achieve success yourself, find partners or allies who can help you. Outsource and delegate if you can afford to hire professional freelancing or consultants.

27.   Know who you want to be in business with whether it is partners, customers or alliances. Define these opportunities on paper if you can.

28.   Allow and trust that your rewards and good will unfold in proportion to you mental energy engaged and tasks performed.

29.   Maintain Consciousness with Causation. Remember to focus on the "Spirit of the Universe" which can also be called the: Impersonal Source and the Framework of the Universe. Keep in tune with this source while cooperating with the impersonal laws of success.

30.   If your mind is devoted to source, the supply of life flows freely. Be aware of the "Spirit of the Universe" within as your supply.

31.   Continue engaging self catharsis, contemplation, clarity, awareness and harmony. Do what works to keep your mind free, clear, relaxed and nimble. In this way, you can create ideas and develop solutions and engage any challenge.

32.   Engage life that prevents giving power to the illusion. The illusion is what negative people think is wrong with the world.

33.   We are not trying to force anything to happen, but rather cooperating and aligning with the laws that can favor us.

34.   Faith Clears the Channel – Faith and belief are the "substances of things unseen" which are the energy that can tilt the cosmic forces in our direction.

35.   The higher and clearer your vibration radiates, the easier it becomes to manifest and create.

36.   Dwell on the realization of your desire and feel the joy of it. Don't get bogged down with unimportant people places or things.

37.   The key is to get clear of mind, get focused, get relaxed, and to contemplate upon the effects and consequences that you want in your life.

38.   Understand and focus on the stimuli that will reward you with the results you desire in your life. Example: A workout in a gym, a how to book, or a reward may actually motivate you or increase your abilities.

39.   Find out what people or businesses you want to be associated with. However, it must be noted that we tend to become more like the people we interact with.

40.   Continue to maintain your harmonious vibration of harmlessness and cooperate with your higher self and maintain your connection to the Spirit of the Universe.

69 Laws of Influence – Read Each Law to Master Your Destiny

To go to the next level, read this book intently, contemplate over the timeless wisdom contained, take action, and become a master of your destiny.

1. Being Well Read – The Guru Bookshelf

First of all, it seems many leaders and billionaires are well read, and stay sharp and maintain a bit of healthy paranoia. They seem to be a type of people to stay very, very informed and dedicate time every day to catching up on the news, debriefing on different issues that are going on whether it's in the press or media, radio, television. And they seem to want to talk to a lot of people so they can keep their fingers on the pulse of their business, humanity and society because they are very interested in their people and very interested in the success of their companies, but also the success of their customers worldwide.

Many of the common themes in the books by billionaires are about leading, about surrounding yourself with good people, serving your customers and knowing your audience, and how to not be an average person, but to be great. With every particular goal, objective, or task we do have to know what our customer is, what they might want, who the target buyer is, how to build something that's authentic or having value, and not just cheap junk. Further, he is a master of how to appeal to people and to the masses and to the influencers out there, and then how to stick to what we want to do using our conviction and perseverance. Billionaires and Leaders tend to read philosophers, religious leaders, legendary figures, history books. Examples: Von Goethe, Buddha, Schopenhauer, Kant, Aristotle, Pythagoras, Marcus Aurelius, Ben Franklin, Swedenborg, Confucius, Sun Tzu, etc.

The Analytical Mind of a Supercharged Billionaire and Leader
The first thing you want to do is to try and get into the mind of the World Leader, and obviously, they have learned different ways of analytical reasoning over their lifetimes. So, they talks a little bit about multi-faceted focusing or multilevel thinking and that's really just about using both sides of your brain (Left and Right). You hear about people who talk about being able to drive subconsciously using their mind to drive their car, not really thinking about it whether it's a stick-shift or automatic, and then there's the other part of the mind that might be talking on the phone. So, what he's getting at is using both sides of the mind, both the conscious and the subconscious, or the mind and the memory to make logical and intuitive decisions simultaneously. But, many of us know that this is a developed skill when it comes to being a master builder.

2. Being Bold and Authentic

In top selling books on human potential, the gurus talk about staying true to yourself, being authentic, standing up for your constructive beliefs and being purposeful and bold. With many American writers, you can see hints of Ralph Waldo Emerson and von Goethe in their writings. They seem to have been influenced quite a bit by being authentic and truthful and bold and purposeful.

3. Good Routines Good Information

In writings of 21st century billionaires, most successful people practice great routines, stay well informed, read different literature from multiple sources, and seek out different viewpoints. They also use metaphorical thinking in terms of pictures and ideas and words by solving problems with using visualization while also creating solutions with using visualization. That means cultivating great ideas, visualizing great plans, and then restructuring problems to make them broader in a sense. So, that's just looking at problems from different angles and different views and seeing how something would work if you changed a few variables. It is a very architectural and special view that most engineers and scientists would have. But, the analytical skill related to it requires knowledge, skill, experience, and a bit of genius.

4. Staying Ahead in the Game of Life

Supercharged people talk about being prepared for all of your potential customers that are out there, which is a very good point regarding your customer, or your voter, or your buyer. And then he talks a little bit about staying a few steps ahead of the competition.

You're trying to visualize or understand a few moves ahead of the players in the chess game, as they say. Just knowing if you do one move, then what will the other person do? That type of forward thinking.

5. Get Your Mind Right – Focus and Confidence

Winners also want people around them to have a focused mind with confidence. A mind that is not a "house divided against itself" Many successful folks use self-affirmation or auto-suggestion and recommend telling yourself that you are brilliant and that you have creative genius. Test it out for yourself by just seeing if this type of internal-statement changes your mindset and be more open minded to see future potentials of the ups and downs of the world. This is not a delusional tactic but rather a tactic to build your mind skills and analytical thinking so you do not limit yourself.

6. Know the Rules, Play Fair, and Win with a Positive Mindset

Great business people talk generously about playing fair and trying to be a decent person with integrity and treating others like you want to be treated. However, these same superstars say you have to keep a strong shield up and protect yourself, and protect your energy, and keep your own positive wavelength or positive mindset. And don't let other people's static, bitterness, or just distractions take you off of your game, because you've got to stay in control of your game. So, don't take other people personally when a lot of times it's just business or like any sporting match, where it's really not personal but about winning under the rules at hand.

7. Boldness with Humility

In many success bestsellers writings, the whole theme is about getting out of your comfort zone, going the extra mile, take healthy risks, and encourages us to not take ourselves too seriously. And there's a lot of literature out there that says you shouldn't take yourself too seriously, that you have to keep one foot in reality, the other in humility while keep focused on determination, persistence and sincerity, but consciously, one must maintain enough humility to keep our eyes open and stay aware of what's going on.

8. Capitalize on Your Assets and Skills

Top performers consistently talk about capitalizing on your skills, your efforts, and your successes. You need to capitalize on those things where your best talents can be maximized, and to continuously improve your results that you achieve, whether it's in business or family or personal life or athletic life, and then avoid complacency.

That doesn't mean to just stay paranoid; it means more just to stay fit spiritually, physically, and bodily. And then to maintain your productivity levels, maintain your enthusiasm, and sometimes you just have to stop and take a moment in life and look at what's out there and just say, "Hey, it's a beautiful world. It's a beneficent universe. Good things can happen."

9. Beat to Your Own Drum

Sometimes you just can't spend your whole life keeping up with the Joneses and we need to beat to your own drum, and keep your own momentum, and just learn to get into your zone and be who you're supposed to be. And respond to life according to who you are, authentically. And work hard, but allow things to come naturally with synchronicity.

10.   Stay Sharp and Agile

And sometimes you have to RE-TOOL and re-motivate yourself for success, but the key is really is just to stay on track, and keep moving, and don't let things slip through your fingers and get lazy.

11.   Know Thyself

It is fairly obvious that top performers believe that we are a product of our: culture, upbringing, self-education, cronic-thinking, and makeup. Even greats such as Dr. Carl Jung believed that we all have embedded talents and desires. As an example, President Obama wrote and spoke much of his ethnic makeup, ancestry and childhood religious upbringing, and even President Trump talks sometimes about his family and his Scottish mother, Mary MacLeod Trump, and he quotes her as saying, "Trust in God and be true to yourself" which are two very important things. So, sometimes leaders such as Trump say that you have to do something if it matters. You've got to do something if it matters to you, if it's important to you, and to be bold and to be authentic, and to be true to your core beliefs.

12.   Ready, Aim, Fire

We all have faced obstacles, enemies, competitors and arguments. Top performers imply that we should pick our challenges carefully, and to pick your aim; choose your chief purpose, your chief aim in life, and commit to it until you finish. There's a many P's that success gurus talks about in their books: purpose, poise, patience, perseverance – all of these concepts are important, because all of us have different goals in life, whether it's a small goal or a big goal, but it's good to learn to commit to something and never look back, and to finish it as best you can. Moreover, the drive for the other P's can be both constructive and destructive; thus, we should all be careful for our question for: Popularity, Power, Prestige, Passion, and Pesos. Even T Boone Pickens, who I also met once many years ago, says that we should get ready, aim and FIRE, and not to sit around waiting to pull the trigger.

13.   Follow Your Heart and Passion to Authenticity

For example, Ralph Waldo Emerson is famous for talking about the power of your ideas which are the greatest part of your mind where you can put these ideas into action to help humanity. Further, Emerson really talked a lot about not following the crowd so much; not being a part of the herd, but to try being true to yourself. Whether you're an individualistic type person with individualistic type of ideas, you can have a valuable contribution without just following the crowd. You can pick your own mission, chose your own destination, and be authentically successful doing what you love. When I was a young man, I sat next to Truet Cathy by accident on a commercial flight. Mr. Cathy told me about his chicken sandwiches. He skillfully sold me on his great company. A few days after the flight, I received a letter from him with some gift cards. He was a true salesman and a real believer in his purpose. It is said that he did more for charity and orphans than any almost other American in history.

14.   Loyalty and Excellence is Always Recognized

Great leaders appreciate loyalty and emphasize being loyal as a: leader, a follower, a worker, a staffer, or even an upper-level person. An intelligent and loyal person will be recognized, but you've got to remember that some of us aren't built for certain types of companies or jobs. That's just the way it is as not all of us are built for a certain job or organization. The famous management consultant Peter Drucker said, "If you work for a large organization for a few years you'll know whether or not you're built for it." Thus, keep your integrity, and people will judge you by your actions.

15.   The World is Constantly Changing

Adapt to the flux. Great leaders teach about opportunity and ideas and preparation, and all of us should be ready for chaos and change. Because there's always going to be ups and downs and there's always going to be chaos, sometimes when there's chaos there is opportunity. When there's an opportunity out there and you meet it with being prepared, that's when real genius and real luck occurs. However, remember that sometimes the road ends or changes, and we need to learn to: re-brand ourselves, re-tool ourselves, keep reinventing ourselves and keep retraining ourselves. We've got to keep showing up and doing our best.

16.   How Will You Contribute Best?

Really, with all of that in mind, it's easier to succeed then it is to fail; because if you take care of yourself and do the right thing, good things will happen. In the twenty-first century economy, we all need to be focusing on how we can make your best contributions to the community, to humanity in general.

Your contribution could be from selling some tool, or product, or service to help people have better lives, or saves lives, but sometimes we have to be realistic and just do our bread-and-butter work so we can take care of ourselves, be self-reliant, and take care of our loved one. Many leaders emphatically says that we've got to keep our passions and hobbies. We can do the things on nights and weekends that we love to do outside of the scope of our general day-to-day work.

17.   Focus on Producing while Keeping Healthy Hobbies.

So, let go of the distractions. Just because you love music, or love a certain sport, love golf – it doesn't mean you can make money at it. There are just some people who are going to be better no matter what, but you can play golf, you can play music, you can do all you want, you can travel, but we do need to focus on how we can best serve the world with our talents and our abilities.

I remember being in the gym one morning in New Orleans in the early 1990s. I was on a renewed health kick and working out hard. As I walked into the gym it was just me and one giant man. We talked and worked out for 45 minutes. Nobody else was there and it was a bit strange. Later that morning, I discovered that I worked out with Magic Johnson, but nobody was there because they were fearful of catching his HIV. In retrospect, it is amazing that they have found treatments to make diseases very manageable. Maintaining our health is vitally important, and once we find out we have a problem, it is important to do all we can to take care of ourselves. Today, Mr. Johnson is more successful than ever.

18.   Learn To Finish Well with Continuous Improvement

If you're new to success, or you're young, or you're starting over, or you're just starting out, gurus like T Harv Eker discuss: getting out there, just learning to do something, getting into your groove, and learn to finish something. Just commit to something and finish the job and do it well. And everyone knows that once you've done something for 30 days, or 60 days, whether it's going to the gym or running a race or whatever it might be, when you finish the finish line, you've done something. If you've completed some task, or built something, whether it's building a fence or digging a ditch and doing a great job – it doesn't matter. The top performers talk about the seed of success and completion creates a new energy, this new flow, this new momentum, and that has to be looked at very keenly, very seriously.

 You think about your ideas and you act on the good ones. Peak performers say that once you finish something, then you have to move on to the next chapter in life, and you have to think about ideas and sit still and maybe get some inspiration from your mind or talk to other people and try to be inspired, but be excited about life; be eager – eager to learn, eager to do, ask questions, ask yourself questions, ask other people questions.

19.   What Would You Do?

What would you want to do next? What do you want to do with your free time? What would you do if you couldn't fail? Success gurus suggest asking ourselves these types of questions (or tells people to ask themselves these types of questions): As some billionaires have said, What lies behind you? What's in front of you?

What are your goals/plans?   What is calling for action within you?
Do you have enough on the inside of knowledge and experience
and willpower? Do you know how your dreams may evolve?

20.   Intuition and Serendipity.

Even leaders such as President say that you have to just allow life to
guide you in different directions. Sometimes you might get caught
on a plane, or a train, or held up in some way, and you're sitting next
to somebody and you start talking and all of a sudden you find out
the greatest new idea, or you find out what's going on in the real
world that some nugget of information that you need to know. So,
sometimes when you are guided, or when things are changed,
sometimes you have to be aware and look for the symbols, the signs,
the information and be aware of your surroundings just in case
something is trying to be presented to you. So, this is really about
cultivating a little intuition, taking advantage of your higher
perception, and maybe allowing a little adventure to create
opportunity in your life.

21.   Importance of Self Reliance and Maximizing Your Potential

On a more personal note, it appears that through the years of
teaching and writing books and trying to help people maximize their
potential, most self help gurus tend to develop a strong belief in self-
reliance from a standpoint of the more people that are self-reliant,
the better it is for the community; the better it is for the churches,
and the hospitals, and the schools; the better it is for the country as a
whole. Thus, the more people that are able to take care of
themselves will result in more people getting taken care of who are
in need.   So, that's the real focus here is that he wants people to be
rich, wealthy, in body, mind and spirit for the benefit of all.

22.   Knowledge and Specific Literacy is Power

The Guru philosophy revolves also around financial and regulatory literacy and like many self-help writers, Real Leaders will talk about staying a student and continuing to be financially literate, success literate, self-help literate, and literate with regards to health, and body, mind, and soul. So, he constantly talks about the more knowledge and experience you have, the better off you will be and the better decisions you'll be able to make.

23.   Change Provides Opportunity

Writers like Paul Zane Pilzer, T Harv Ekar, Tony Robbins, Larry Kudlow, and many other great people out there talk about how every time that a huge collapse or a huge change occurs in society – that there's lessons to be learned and we learn how to react, how to reinvest, how to re-tool, how to regroup.

With the crash of 2000, we learned that technology wasn't invincible at that time. It took 16 years for the stock market to come back from the Clinton Crash, which was the greatest stock market crash in history. The second biggest crash is the one that happened in 2008, 2009, when Bush was transferring power to Obama.

In this chaos, we can learn a lot about real estate, a lot about risk, a lot about investments, and you've got to take a hard look at your investments and what's inside of those investments and know what the costs and fees are and know what you're investing in. You can't just put your money is some fund and not know what it's about. The other thing is sometimes economies change and substitutes are created. Now, oil and gas might be one example, and we used to import a lot of oil and gas from other countries, now we're becoming more and more self-reliant, but when one industry sector changes, then we all need to learn how to adapt and reinvent and prevail. As an example, when energy is cheap, inflation slows, people in transportation make big money, and disposable income for the people increases. Thus, while Oil and Gas Superpowers may make a little less, the dollars go to other places where opportunities for investment presents itself.

24.   Good Instincts – A Skill To Be Harnessed

One of the interesting words that some self help masters use is the word prescience. It looks like "pre-science." Really, this word is about having great instinct or taking advantage of a gut feeling or ideas that come from the inside. This is not necessarily about knowing the future but just having good instincts about what decisions to make to increase the potentiality of success.

He talks about how experience, knowledge, intuition and inspiration are a great combination of mental powers. If you have learned experience and you've developed good knowledge from education where you also try and cultivate quiet time where you can mentally be aware of your subconscious and your conscious mind, all of these things come together and allow you to be a very powerful thinker and a powerful decision-maker.

With such as dynamic world of new technology and global interactions, we must be aware when one door closes and another door is open and be willing to learn from opportunities and mistakes and being aware of detours and being able to take a preemptive strike huge changes come. These are all great abilities to have.

25.   Self Respect and Self Regard – The Inner Power

We must all cultivate self-respect and self-regard and being confident in ourselves and having a quality ego consciousness with a sense of purpose. What is meant by saying "ego consciousness" is to have a healthy ego, one that can't be belittled or shamed by other people who are jealous of you or don't want you to succeed. But in the end, Most powerful people advocate the art of knowing how to self-promote and knowing how to humbly tell people about your successes and allowing people to know your skills and your arts.

There was a famous book called Brag that I wrote a book review on. It's a good book by Peggy Claus. We all must become our own "Master of the Brag", and Peggy Claus puts this formula in writing.

26.   Teamwork and Public Relations

With any successful person, you become a market leader. To be a market leader, you really need sellable idea, be aggressively truthful, take the high road, and having a great product or service you can believe in. You must learn to be able to promote yourself and promote the other people that are with you. All of this is very, very important to him as the power of a unified and concerted PR stance is very strong.

27.   Great Ideas and Study – Keep Up With Your World

Victor Hugo says that there's one thing stronger than all the armies of the world, and that is an idea whose time has come. Top teachers encourages life-long learning and never looking at education as being a burden. They talk about with any new business or any new task or any new goal, there might be some new type of learning and preparation that might be needed to be done. We must cultivate the ability to think and to use all of your power to maximize and develop the capacity to think.

28.   Thankfulness

Winners and success gurus speak a great deal about gratitude and thanksgiving and having a thankful heart. They often speaks of their parents and siblings with great reverence and love. President Trump even speak of his deceased brother Fred as a great teacher of what NOT to do because before his brother Fred died of alcohol related issues, he asked Donald not to get involved with alcohol and President Trump heeded his brother's wishes.   In the midst of successes and failures and losses, it's extremely important to remain thankful for all the blessings that we've received and all the blessings that we may receive.

29.   Transcendental

With regard to being your best, many success gurus have great respect for some of the founding fathers and transcendentalists authors such as Thoreau and Ralph Waldo Emerson. Really, at its core, I think that most super successful business people are trying to say that we should develop a higher consciousness and use that mental power in tandem with our actions. It's about being contemplative or mindful while being action, and we should be prepared while we are in action.

30.   What is Your Energy Level – How Will It Serve You?

Top gurus like Tim Fariss and Navy Seals are highly revered for energy and work ethic. They say that many over achievers, decide just to put in another three/four hours of work in each day. They figure that performance would change from this extra effort. If you do the math on it, if you put another three/four hours of your day every day, you've basically added another month to your year of productivity. It's an extremely important ideal if you can get by on four/five hours of sleep a day.

31.   Stay Aware and Keep Growing

Masters of high performance also profess at length about the concepts of perception, awareness, and mindfulness. With everything that you do, looking at your strengths, your weaknesses, your opportunities and your threats, never becoming too complacent and always putting in your best effort; always being mindful of when you need to adapt or change or take a detour to try to get over, under or around some obstacle and being concise and to the point in your work and in your presentations, and continuing to learn and continuing to be curious.

True life coaches also talk about Growth, and how we MUST keep growing in body, mind and spirit.   Always be mindful of your growth and your track record. Sometimes growth is painful, and if you go to the gym and you work out really, really hard, you might be in pain the next day but that's what growth is. We need to be vibrant, we need to be open to greatness and we need to be open to success. We must be open to being better and better while maintaining industrious to create more opportunities.   Sometime just by the fact that we're showing up early and leaving late, we're presented with more opportunities than we would have had before. One of the goals that Leaders may be implying is to: seek our uniqueness, our own style, our own beat, our own momentum and to get out of our own comfort zones and just try to do our best.

### 32.	Life as an Art Form

Many leaders of great success see life as an art form. Really, at its core, every business is just like an artist's business. You've got to produce and paint something great that people want, that people are willing to pay for. But then you've got to make sure that people see it because the more people that have access to admire it, the more eyeballs that might see it, the better odds that you'll get paid a fair value for that master creation. This applies to real estate, politics, jewelry, literary works and most all businesses. I remember talking to Claus Obermeyer about necessities. He told me that his wife made a down vest for him to keep him warm; thus, the creation of an ski industry attire and fashion because an immigrant saw the need for certain clothing in the USA. Therefore, the Sport Obermeyer company was born.

### 33.	Wisdom

Wisdom is one of the highest virtues, and even in the Bible, King Solomon becomes the wealthiest man in the world by asking his God for Wisdom. If you have wisdom, you will become wealthy. Wisdom is a combination of experience and knowledge.   There are many great books on wisdom and strategy as Machiavelli's, *The Prince* and *The Art of War* by Sun Tzu.

Another interesting facet about leaders is that they respect their ancestors culture and traditions. Many leaders study their ancestors and understand the talents of their forefathers. People engage self discovery, study their ancestry, and maybe travel to the sacred villages or sites of their ancestors.

And sometimes when you analyze your ancestors, and where you're from, you can learn about the different cultures, and the different mindsets, and the different types of things that people did in these different parts of the world. Moreover, it allows us to study history and to be a student of history; including culture, military history, immigration, and other history.

34.   Don't Be Afraid or Ashamed of Winning

Many, many people are just scared or too timid to allow themselves to be victorious and enjoy it, and to be a good winner. With being a winner, it's about doing a great job one day at a time, being the best you can be "in the now", and it's just one step at a time, one golf stroke at a time, one surf board ride at a time, while understanding your environment and doing your best.

35.   The Now

Another question that luminaries like Dyer, Tolle, or Chopra might ask a seeker is: "What's your mindset?" so that you can analyze your performance each day while paying attention to success. Look at your ability to respond to the world. And again, many masters seem to be emphasizing the importance of the now, and to concentrating all of your efforts on the work at hand, or the task at hand, or what's going on right now and doing your best right now. Remember, the now creates the future and your actions and thinking in the NOW are what drives you toward your destiny.

36. Business Really is an Art Form and Negotiating is Like a Complex Dance With a Partner Who May Not Know How To Dance Like You Do

Doing your homework and being prepared are really nine-tenths of the builder's craft; so, life really is about cultivating your signature craft. If you look at any top author such as Napoleon Hill or Dale Carnegie or Zig Ziglar or any of the other top peak performance authors, they will ask you, "What is your goal? What is your aim? What are you shooting for? What is your vision? What is your 'why'? Why do you want to do something? What is your essence? Why are you doing it?" People sometimes say I want to make X amount of money, but what are you going to do with the money once you get it?

Therefore, it's good to know what you are going to do if you succeed, or how you going to be or live if you succeed. Clarify your intentions, clarify your thoughts, write them out, clarify with your mind your visualizations, and then learn to put it all together and remain well educated and you can synthesize information to take action on a daily basis.

Really, the key here is continuous learning. When you have experience, you have knowledge, you have the ability to see different variables that are going on, you are able to synthesize or combine the information to see a bigger picture.

37. Obstacles

Philosophers and leaders say that sometimes you just can't label something as good or bad or give every obstacle a bad name. Often, we just have to identify an concern or challenge that we need to get around, rather than to fear it with some problematic character.

So, with that being said, we need to break down our concerns of every obstacle into objective issues or pieces and then try and determine a path to success, and we can always compartmentalize each day with focus on the tasks at hand, or compartmentalize the actual obstacle and work to get around it.

And then we need to know what we are getting or doing before we are implementing something. We must to learn to diagnose something to a get a plan and to know how to act before we actually start the action.

To understand the consequences of actions going out for days or even years. So, many philosophical such as the Stoics, Transcendentalist, Native Americans, or the Prosperity Gospel followers really believe that fear feeds a counterproductive part of our mind which is a part of your consciousness that doesn't need to be fed. So, we should replace the weakness attitude with one of power and confidence and faith.

38.   Developing a Big Picture

A mental big picture is the art of using applied visualization. This skill is about learning to focus the mind and to see the potential consequences, the potential outcome of any decision. If you take certain actions what will happen? Better yet, learn to truly see the actual final success in your mind's eye on the picture screen of your imagination. With that being said, that final picture in your mind of success can actually help you develop actionable ideas as well toward the successful end result.

39.   Success is a Combination of Aptitude, Work, and Opportunity, and a Little Good Fortune.

If you always do more than what is expected, and you have acquired the skills that you need to engage in what you want to do, then you will develop a reputation and business art form that people will respect and your creativity will be esteemed. So, we all need to mindful of how to be a: deliberate, focused, intentional person who works smart, and who works hard. Additionally, we should aspire to find our authentic expression in your work, our authentic style, and passion. Be yourself, get the job done, be excellent, be prepared, seek opportunity and providence will be presented to YOU.

40.   One Day at a Time

As a builder of great companies, most billionaires can give a great lecture on getting tasks done, and completing goals, and having the right mindset. And every trained project manager knows that for each goal we must diagnose the problem and put together a plan, and then implement a plan, and then work on each task at hand to implement that plan with focus and responsibility and teamwork. And then be able to self appraise the situation for continuous improvement. Having these skills is important but being able to focus "one day at a time" and "one task at a time" is very important because laser focus and daily achievement add up fast to great successes.

41.   Communications

Having good communications skills and the ability to sit down and explain yourself to another party or to a group of people. And that involves being able to take complex information and distill it down into a way of presenting it to others so that they can all understand what you are saying at a level that all parties can understand. Further, getting to the point and being concise and not beating around the bush is a strong point advocated by any investor from Silicon Valley to Hong Kong. Thus, mastering the art of not wasting time with communications, but actually hitting the points of the target. Some cultures such as the Swiss demand preparation before any meeting; thus, everyone wants to get the facts and have the due diligence completed to learn the most important information in the most effective and efficient way.

42.   Achieving Greatness

Many leaders discuss with emphasis the art of being excellent and achieving greatness. And all great achievements are possible with a positive attitude, with awareness and clarity. But, we must be realistic and seek realistic solutions. With that being said, all great achievements are based on perseverance and having a consciousness of success.   We believe that most successful leaders understand that all people have their own unique style and their own unique flair. Even Google advocated that employees spend a portion of each week toward their passions and toward innovation. If you're going to be an employee within a large organizational chart, naturally you're going to have to do what is asked of you and perform and get results. But, I think the most successful companies are very aware that all people have their own style and their own way of doing things in an excellent way. They can do it pretty much using the same methodology as the masters or other great performers, but they might handle things just a little bit different.

You only need to watch great tennis players like Rafa Nadal or Roger Federer or any of the other greats such as the Williams sisters. It is apparent to us all that each one has their own style, their own flair. Each master has the type of clothes they feel best in, the type of rackets they use, shoes, equipment, mental preparedness, workouts, exercise, and all of that. They even each have their own rituals before during and after their games. Moreover, they play their best using their own game; they don't play other people's games.

43.   Self Appraisal

With every winner, there is a process of self inventory, and I think that leaders from Ben Franklin to Napoleon Hill and Dr. Stephen Covey all try to look at people and convey a message that each person should try and develop and create a track record of positive results that they may improve upon. It's almost like a resume or a curriculum vitae, you're trying to build assets, and respectable achievements, a quality track record, and positive results. And you should be able to itemize those things; write them down, list them and be able to articulate them to others so you can maximize your highest talents and VALUE.

44.   Quiet Time, Mindfulness and Contemplation

Some of the most powerful leaders advocate retreats to rest or bond with groups. Many of the most successful believe in quiet reflection and recharging the spirit. This can be done each day for a few minutes or each year. Generally, all of us need to take time to unplug and have peaceful time to relax or meditate or sit still. It seems like most gurus are accentuating the fact that we can take time each day to relax and to quiet our mind to seek inspiration and to tune into the power of the mind and the universe.

And this is the way that many great thinkers, whether its Edison or Einstein, have been able to sit down and decipher problems, or come up with new ideas to solve big challenges, or get around big obstacles.

The greats practice contemplation by sitting down and allowing your brain, your conscious and your subconscious, to do some of the work for you.

45.   Momentum and Authenticity

If you read about Lincoln, Roosevelt, Emerson and Thoreau and other great writers, we learn that we have to be authentic, be ourselves, and listen to our heart. We should be authentic but be effective. In essence, we must do all things well each day. And if you do 3 things well each day, that adds up to momentum, and at the end of the year you've done 1,000+ things great. Thus, this is a part of thinking big and thinking of the long term while being patient.

46.   Persistence

We all know the story of the tortoise and the hare. The slow steady turtle beats the fast creature in a race by taking one methodical step at a time and focusing on the mission and destination. Thus, being able to just find out what you need to start early, try and finish early, and try and maintain a sustainable, effective way of doing things in a reasonable way and not involving waste IS a path to success.

Know what your creative assets are and use them to the best of your ability. Know what makes you valuable to yourself and others and use those attributes to be the most determined person in your field.

47.   Your Legacy

Have you ever targeted or itemized what do you want to be known for? This is something that Ben Franklin talked about over 200 years ago by focusing on excellence. It's something Dr. Stephen Covey of the "7 Habits" talked about just a few years ago in his bestsellers. You legacy is: what do you want people to say about you when you're gone? What do you want to be known for? Do you want to be known for somebody who's sober, sharp, and upright. Or you want to be known as somebody who's unfit and smokes and drinks too much. This is just an example.

48.   Inspiration

If we learn to use instinct with inspiration and logic, we can really approach great genius in word and deed.

So, you use your mind and your gut. Utilize your consciousness, your sub consciousness, and your gut instincts. While many great leaders refer to instincts in the same way that some of us might refer to intuition, it's sort of the same thing. Sometimes we just get that feeling and we know what we are supposed to do. And I think that's what Trump is talking about.

And if you can learn how to use all those thinking powers simultaneously, that can help you be a great person. And most success writers say that most of us are only using a small portion of our mind power. And really developing the use of your consciousness, your sub consciousness, and your instincts, and your inspiration, and intuition, all those things together can help you act accordingly in the now.

49.   Art of the Sale

And Mr. Trump does talk, again, a lot about marketing and I think it's because his whole life he's been involved in preparing buildings and services to be sold to those who need housing or golf or other things, and providing them with the attributes of a product or service that the customer wants. Whether its building safety or security and a good business location and all the accoutrements you would need.

And so, a lot of what he's talking about is getting to the common denominator of what people really want, particularly smart people or affluent people and relating this common denominator to the audience and to the customers and being able to explain, "This is what's best for you," and why, and finding out who your target is and targeting those people.

Honestly, he talks a lot about how life is an art form and being able to convey that art to other people in the best way is one path to great success. Like they say, even a great artist is willing to reproduce a great piece that looks similar to one before it if it has such great appeal to the best people.

50.   Chaos and Catastrophe

Mr. Trump does use some metaphors and allegories to describe some of his thoughts on success. And since some of his books were written after calamities such as the great stock market crash of 2000 during the Clinton Administration, the 911 Attacks on New York, and then the following stock market crash during the Bush Administration, transition to Obama in 2008 and 2009.

Mr. Trump talks a lot about the need to maintain poise and calm when chaos comes. And to be prepared for when that chaos comes and have some ideas of maybe some chess moves you might make if something bad happens.

It's called a preemptive strike. Even great Olympians will sometimes prepare for the worst if something happens to me during my competition. For example, if equipment malfunctions, how am I going to deal with that.

And the same way with any great entrepreneur is that being prepared, staying calm, maintaining your humility, not fighting against the forces that are out there, adapting as best you can, and then seizing opportunities.

Everybody probably who's reading this or listening to this knows that there's people out there that have made fortunes after the collapse of the economy, buying real estate or after an S&L bailout they went out and bought a bunch of apartments and did great. This is the same thing, you seize these opportunities. But, not fighting situations is also a key.

Thus, Trump articulates that when we are prepared as opportunity presents itself, this is equivalent to luck. And, a lot of great writers talk about, chaos is always equivalent to opportunity for many people and if you're prepared for chaos and opportunity, then that's when great things happen.

51.   Street Credibility

Trump has some sage advice about building your street credibility and your reputation and your integrity. And there's several steps to this that President Trump talks about, but a few of them include being a continuous learner and building your intelligence. Learing to focus in an area and becoming a specialist. Being responsible and having the ability to respond to situations, and then being loyal either to yourself or to your company or to the people you work for. Being authentic and being a results oriented person where good is not good enough; it has to be better than that.

## 52.	Getting Rich

Everyone wants to know how to get rich and President Trump's views are much in line with the views of many entrepreneurial Americans and bestselling authors. Trump teaches that a lot of our ability to become prosperous is in the mind and its cultivating the mental powers of being able to think, and act, and do with informed intelligence while keeping your mind persistent, and keeping the momentum.

But, President Trump is very clear about finding out what you want to do and what your purpose is. And if anyone has ever read the books by Ralph Waldo Emerson or Carl Jung or other great authors and visionaries, they know that we can all be best at certain things. So, we can all perform better doing certain things more in line with our passions and desire. Many top management consultants say we all have unique & innate talents, drives and desires.

Thus, if you maintain a positive mindset, and can work hard, and learn, and do the right thing, and maintain your reputation of results and integrity you're probably going to do well in life.

But again, if you've read books by Napoleon Hill and other great writers, they talk about what is your purpose and you need to find out what that purpose is, what you really want to do, and how you want to do it, and head in that direction, and don't look back. And that's really about your burning desires, your chief aim or your chief purpose.

And then, when you find out what your chief aim in life is, your work will become a labor of love; it could be being the best writer, or the best teacher, the best golf player, it doesn't matter When you find out what that is then you devote your time and you focus on that, and you work as efficiently and as effectively as you can, and you use action, and you maintain your pace, you maintain your time management, and you focus on your work, and you maintain your momentum, and you finish the job, and you do it to the best of your ability. You will maximize your potential and excellence.

Mr. Trump also talks about the skills needed to become wealthy and prosperous and successful. A lot of that has to do with the ability to work with other people and to cultivate relationships, to reach out, to ask, to knock on the door, to receive when someone offers you something. All of these things are pretty obvious, but President Trump talks a lot about keeping the right people, and the right places, and the right things in your orbit so they can help you and you can help them and give back.

53.   Tithing, Charity and Flow

One of the things about Mr. Trump that's not talked about is his unbelievable dedication to charity, and giving back, and tithing. And there's many people like Trump out there, whether it's Oprah Winfrey or the great Truett Cathy of Chick-fil-A who gave 10% his entire life, and people like the Carnegie's that gave great money to charity to build the US Library System.

All of these people did great works, and it seems like Trump does the same thing. He, much like Oprah Winfrey, just doesn't advertise or promote the fact that he continues to give to charity. Whether it's to hospitals, or churches, or temples, or schools, or to those individuals in need who need medical care, he always seems to have a track record of tithing to people and communities that divinely inspire him.

54.   Labor of Love – Going the Extra 1%

President Trump reiterates being specific with your intentions, knowing your purpose and finding a labor of love. He speaks of discovering your passion, trying to outwork others, and having fun doing it. Similarly, as great authors like Zig Ziglar talk about, the difference between a great success and a failure can be 1% or 2% extra effort.

So, if you always put in an extra little 1% or 2% a day, you're probably going to outsmart the rest of the people, particularly if you're doing a good job and effective and efficient type of performance. So, finding out what your passion is. What's your blueprint look like? What do you want to do? Whether its medicine, or law, or sports, or technology, it doesn't matter. It's just finding out what makes you enthusiastic, what makes you feel ALIVE, and what energizes you.

55.   The Builder – All Creation Begins with an Idea

And as you remember, many leaders are mental builders at heart. And all of us out there, whether you're building websites or building schools, it's all a different type of artwork, all a different type of creation. So, when you build things you have to think about what's at stake there and how do you make quality. How do you create value? How do you create increase for the buyer?

If you've read great self-help authors from over the last hundred years, they talk about the law of increase and I really think Trump has got a lot of that in his DNA where he wants to provide amazing things for people. And if they pay a lot more than what's expected, it's because they feel like their lives are increasing as a result of what the builer is providing. And that's the real signature of a real leader which is being able to build things that people really want or are willing to pay a little extra for.

56.   Empathy with Energy

Trump talks about being compassionate, and empathetic, and using the powers that you have to be kindhearted towards others but staying hungry for excellence. He talks about staying aggressive and keeping that underdog mindset. Be confident, yeah, but always keep that underdog mindset and make sure you understand who and what you're competing against.

And even in this day and age, you may not just be competing against your neighbor down the street or some guy from another state; you might be competing with other people from 180 different countries. And in the end, when you deal with other people, or you deal with customers or buyers, you're trying to create win-win deals where mutual compromise sometimes is the best way to get closure on any deal.

57.   Trust but Verify – Keep the Keys to the City

This section is about hiring good people. I mean hire the best people you can. Incentivize great employees or affiliates, do great things for them, make sure they want to work with you and be a part of the team.

Make sure they're team players if you can by giving them clear rules of the game and a path to win. If they're not team oriented players, make sure they've got skills that they can share with the organization that are valuable.

More importantly, you've got to have backstops and protection on everything related to your business, property, risk, and finances. You just can't trust people with the keys to the city. So, make sure you're in control of your bank accounts, make sure you're in control of your passwords. Make sure you're in control of your email. Make sure you're in control of your: agreements, accounts, rental space, registrations, even domain names, and on down the line.

If somebody has too much access to your customer information, your technology, and your trade secrets, they can make a move and take advantage of that, and take advantage of your network, take advantage of your money. So, hire great people, but be careful and make sure you have control over the key assets, and insure that nobody can hijack them just by walking out the door, and starting a new company that looks just like yours.

58.   Goals, Objects and Ideals – Being Mindful of the Essence

Anybody can have a goal with a money number on it and say, " I want to be a millionaire, or I want to make $100,000 this month", or whatever it is. Anybody can make up a financial goal with a number, and that's a good idea to have an in life's game which includes: an exact number or a specific result, but on a metaphysical level, it's much more important to know the essence behind the number.

So, there's an old story that somebody prayed for $10,000 and soon thereafter, they were hurt on the job in an accident, and the injured got a $10,000 severance check. So, the moral of the story is be careful what you pray for.

Pray or be Mindful for something specific, but understand what you're going to do to receive this reward. Like, I want to help 10,000 people get a better education, and learn how to be better people, and reach their human potential. And by helping these 10,000 people, I'm going to make a million dollars doing it. And, that's generally what is meant by the essence behind what you want. You can imagine yourself completing a task or finishing a race, or whatever it is, and that's perfect, but you have to understand what you are going to do when I finish the job, or how am I going to finish the job successfully, and who am I going to help along the way or afterward in relation to this particular goal or task or objective.

59.   Life Changing Event

Another excellent point that is made by people who follow Trump's teachings is the fact that: any one event, or any one victory in life can change your life forever and make you a PLAYER. And, the teaching is that: "You need to become that Event", or be "at one with" that turning point in your life, and target" a passion, excellence, or a dream that is going to put you in the big league.

60.   Brutal Honesty and Tough Love is Required Sometimes

This section really is about the reality of the world, and the fact of the matter is that if you become successful, there's going to be people that admire you, and they're going to people that hate you no matter what. It doesn't matter where you go in life, whether you are a child or adult, when you walk into an establishment, there are going to be some people that just don't like the way you look, but there's going to be some people that love the way you look. It doesn't really matter. That's not the point we're trying to make. The point is that in the end, there's always going to be somebody who is jealous of you, or wants what you have, wants: your car, or your clothing, or your loved ones, or your job, it doesn't really matter.

Once you start moving up the food chain there's people at the bottom of the food chain that are going to look at you like a target, and there's going to be mean and smart people who are going to try and separate you from your success and your money, and your happiness, and that's one of the other key things is you really need to do is to: protect your body, and your mind, and your soul.

You need to learn how to protect your mindset (in some countries, they might say to protect your Energy). This is because all great people, all successful people have a powerful mind and a powerful brain, but you need to protect it from these people who want to suck your energy, and take from you, and not give you something of value in return.

So, really, the high level operating people, people that are operating at a higher level mentally, know how to protect their mind and their heart from problem people, and at least try to avoid toxic situations. And, many self-help gurus out there will say that half of life's luck is avoiding:: bad people, and bad places, and bad things, and toxic situations. It's just a fact that avoiding belligerent imbeciles and other traps is half of life's luck.

61.   Make Your Reputation as a Fighter Known

Another fascinating point that people like President Trump and other's make is that you have to know how to be an open minded person, and a person who listens, and that is helpful in business, but you can't be a pushover either.

So, the point of the lesson here is that: you can't be other people's doormat. And if you're in a competitive business where there's a lot of other businesses competing for the same thing, you really have to know how to defend yourself. And, not take crap from other people. And, the moral of the story is if somebody does something wrong to you, and you have a cause of action, you need to get a lawyer or report it to the authorities, and you need to take care of it.

And, you need to make sure other people know that you're not going to be the type of person to take some abusive situation from another person. If somebody tries to sue you for instance and you're in the right and they're in the wrong more than you, let's say you're in the wrong, and they're in the wrong, but they're in the wrong <u>much more</u> than you, you countersue and you hit them with everything you've got. You hit them with as many charges and as many counts, and as many claims as you can. You try and hit them for compensatory damages and for punitive damages and treble damages. You get it filed in court, and it becomes public and it makes your opponent look very bad particularly if you have a good case. Even if the offender is in Australia or China, you find a way to assert jurisdiction over the offenders and make them pay and drag them into court in the USA.

That's just the legal world that we're in. Never let other people get one over on you, particularly if you have the edge and leverage. Now, somebody comes at you and they're suing you, and they clearly have all the leverage, then figure out how to get out of the case as quickly as you can and settle it with a win-win deal, particularly if it's going to be a waste of your time and energy, and you'll be spinning your wheels. But there's some cases that are just crap, you'll know the difference, but don't let some "run of the mill lawyer" convince you that you have a good case unless you really do.

62.   Make People Happy to Work for You

There are many ways to inspire people. No matter what business you're in, whether you're a doctor or you're a lawyer, or you're selling clothes, or selling books, or whatever it is, it doesn't matter.

There's going to be other people helping if you want to be GREAT, and you'll want to try and help other people to help you sell and promote this business, or this product, or this service that you have. And, the more people you have helping you, the more eyeballs that might see your product or service are the possibility that you have for selling things and making an honest living and helping people by getting your product and service in other people's hands, and you receive some type of compensation for it.

So, the logic behind all of this is that: you've got figure out how to incentivize people if you can. If there's a way to split, give everybody a commission on something that they're selling for you, DO IT. As they say in many a countries in Asia and other places, if there's a way to cut somebody a little margin, DO IT. If people are working hard, you will want them to be emotionally involved in helping you. Basically, margin means commission, or a little percentage, and if there's a way to cut them in, do it.

And, that's how Amazon Google and all these other internet companies have became so big. Basically, for many years during the internet growth, internet companies had a lot of people doing what's called affiliate sales, and having somebody promote their little products and services and links and pages and everything with free advertising, and they give resellers a little piece.

And after a couple of years, internet companies let's go a lot of these people and got rid of certain reselling mechanisms with led to commission based sale. Thus, much of the marketing for the internet greats was done by little people on the ground.   I'm just saying that "free and incentivized marketing a big. It is the same with brokers or insurance companies who will hire agents to boost PR to family and friends. If they are successful, you keep them; if not, let them go.

And if anybody does an excellent job, and if anybody's really selling whether it's for Amazon or Google or anybody else, if anybody's really selling for them, making them money, they're going to buy you out. And, they're going to make sure you get paid, particularly if you're doing a great job. So, it's a two sided street, and if you can do a good job, that's how you can become rich - because in any sales position, it's an untold, unlimited amount of possibilities.

63.   Get It in Writing – Think Ahead – Exit and Risk Strategy

Now, we are talking about protecting yourself with legal documentation. And, it doesn't matter if it's just family or spouse as a lot of people talk about prenuptial agreements and protecting yourself in marriage, and all that. That's fine. If your husband or wife or whatever wants to sign, or fiancée wants to sign one of these things, that's fine. A lot of people bring assets into the marriage whether they inherit it or not. Those things belong to you, but you might want to find ways to protect separate assets as well through some type of agreement or keep it separate under the local and state laws that allow separate property to be kept.

But, there's lots of other LEGAL documentation that's just as important. If you're in a partnership with someone else in business, whether it's in services, restaurant, small business, law or medicine or insurance, or whatever it is, if you have some partner, you're going to want to have a prenuptial "Business" agreement with these people that you work with.

And, it's not called a prenuptial agreement, of course, but it might be called a buyout agreement, operating agreement or something of the sort. If your partner dies or whatever, you get a chance to buy out their stock. Or, have some mechanism in place where you can buy out the shares or have right of first refusal, whether it's in an LLC document or a corporate document, these types of terms can be added.

And particularly with family, if you've ever studied wealth management or listened to a financial management lecture, everybody needs to have a will, maybe a living will, a healthcare directive etc. Thus, there's all these things to protect you or your loved ones in case you're incapable of managing your affairs, and you need someone else to do it for you, or if you become sick.

And then, there's other things like that might be a really smart move for you is make sure you can buy health insurance. If you're healthy buy life insurance. If you're healthy try and get some disability insurance if you can afford it because you never know what's going to happen. There's a certain amount of risk out there no matter what. Your health is the most important thing.

64.   Get Quality and Buy 1ˢᵗ Class if You Can

The next section is just about buying QUALITY. And, anybody who's reading or listening right now remembers going to the store during your life, and you looked at an expensive pair of shoes, and then you looked at another pair of shoes that was a little less, and you bought the pair of shoes that was a little less. And, in the end the pair of shoes that was a little less didn't look quite as good, didn't last quite as long, and certainly weren't comfortable enough on your feet, and I mean, sometimes you better just go ahead, and buy a $300 or $400 pair of shoes, or $900 pair of shoes. I don't know what a great ladies shoe costs, however, great handmade shoes start out probably $300, $400 in cash right now in 2017.

I remember back when I was a young law student working in a building in downtown, working downtown, and there was an old attorney there who had some custom made shoes from London, and one pair was 22 years old, and another pair was 25 years old, and they still looked brand new. He had them shined and conditioned at least once a month and took them off the moment he got home. He had them custom fit where he had some company make a mold of his foot in London, and he had the shoes mailed to him, you know, every 10 years he had a new pair, or something, unbelievable.

The same holds true with a nice belt, a nice jacket, a nice care, a nice suit, and on and on it goes, and even Mr. Trump uses a story about buying some sports team that is valuable. He says, if you buy, go for the big league and get a hold of a real team that's first rate, you know, whether it's an NFL or an NBA team, and it's always going to have value because market leaders always maintain their value. And, the same holds true with the property. If you're in a great part of town, whether you're in the smallest house or the largest house, those well situated properties usually maintain their value.

65.   Your Image and Brand

The last part is just about being a high level person: in the way you speak, the way you handle yourself, the way you hold yourself up, the type of people you surround yourself with where all of these attributes are incredibly important.

Further, not everybody has the ability to look perfect. But certainly, taking care of yourself, taking care of your body, taking care of your hair and your teeth, and your skin and everything else is very, very important.

I mean it just, this goes back to like the old story of the Beatles, you know, back when they were starting out, you know, the manager went out and got them some nice outfits and made them look good and cleaned them up, and that's just, you know, the way it is, and the flipside of that is whether, you know, any rock and roll star will tell you back when he was young, he wanted to hire an agent who looked good, drove a nice car, and had a nice suit.

 It's just the same old story, and most people don't want their lawyer, priest or doctor to look weird or drive an old broken down car. They want their agents and employees and bosses to look good, fit the part, and look like a success It's just the way of the world. So, the moral of the story is to think of yourself as important. Believe you're important, and organize yourself like you're important.

66.   What's My Value – What Have You Done For Yourself Lately?

The hardest thing to do is taking a hard look at yourself, and each year or every six months or every year you have to take a hard look at yourself and take an inventory and find out what makes you worth a lot to other people. What are your top hobbies, and talents, and knowledge that you have? And how are you willing to use these things to better your community and humanity and make your life better for you and your loved ones?

And then, being bold and being proactive, getting out of your comfort zone, taking steps to make your life better and to improve yourself. Moreover, being objective, and listening to other people, and maybe asking for other people's opinions about how to go forward.

And then, keeping your eyes open and aware to the changes in society and humanity, whether its new products and services, or whether it's with your particular city or state, or whether it's with a different country around the world, or the different needs of people from around the world that are coming. All these might provide different opportunities for you to provide your human capital and your value to other people.

And in the end, to sum up this little section on my understanding of the President and his mindset is you have to try and learn who you are. Know thyself, but also know who your people are that are helping you and what their capacities are, and know how to talk to them and know how to ask them to be their best. But also, knowing how to synthesize or synergize information or your actual assets for the best results; really taking into consideration all the different variables around you, whether it's in a negotiation or the completion of a project on a day-to-day basis, or to actually maybe meeting your goals at the end of the year, or the end of five years, or the end of ten years.

67.   The Art of Any Deal

1. Know who is involved – The parties
2. Know the purpose of the deal
3. Know the terms
4. Know who does what – Who is responsible for implementing the deal

5. How long is the deal?
6. What is the Bargain? Who pays want.
7. Understand the how and when to assent to the deal and make it a meeting of the minds where the agreement is binding.
8. Is the deal insured or protected.
9. Know how to get out of the deal.
10.   Know how the deal is protected from harm, injury, or insured etc. What is your exit strategy of selling or moving on.
11.   Aim high in asking for what you want and more and be willing to settle the deal on mutually beneficial terms.
12.   Be Flexible: Trump says, ""I never get too attached to one deal or one approach," Trump writes. "For starters, I keep a lot of balls in the air, because most deals fall out, no matter how promising they seem at first. In addition, once I've made a deal, I always come up with at least a half dozen approaches to making it work, because anything can happen, even to the best-laid plans."
13.   Know your market
14.   Find leverage and use it.
15.   Keep the deal sustainable with costs.
16.   Fight for what you want.
17.   The deal is to create quality services or products. Thus, you must be able to deliver value.

68.   Working Hard – Having Great Energy and Winning

How did President Trump Win? Whether you know it or not, President Trump visited 4, 5 or more cities a day during the campaign. What people did NOT SEE, is that he sat down with THOUSANDS of people and asked questions to find out what was wrong, what needed to be done, how can we improve this country. Yet, another reason he won a majority 30 states which was better than even Obama's record of 28 states. He won by listening and outworking his opponents.

And overall, the synergy and the power of the whole shined true on November 8, 2016, when Mr. Trump won the presidential election. They gave him an 8% chance of winning. He won over 30 states in the United States, a majority of 30 different provinces, when his opponent only won 20 different provinces.

It was a major victory and a major upset of both here and worldwide. The shockwaves were felt worldwide and the power of these ideas and concepts speak to how and why he won.

Even in Trump's book credits, you see references to Dr Norman Vincent Peale who was the master of the "Power of Positive Thinking". Knowing these influences, Trump kept a positive attitude from the very beginning of his campaign. He didn't let the naysayers and the people who insulted him to slow down his momentum. He constantly worked with others to find out how to be his best. He constantly looked at his target audience, which is the voter and the people, to find out what their needs were and to try and articulate policies and ideas that would help them feel better about voting for him and electing him as President of the United States of America.

69.   Luck and Haminja

Another interesting thing about a WINNING Mindset is that some people are just a little bit luckier than others, believe in themselves just a little bit more, and believe in their abilities a tad more than others. And if you've ever studied EurAsian Mythology, there's some tribes in the North, like in the old Norse mythology where the ancient people's believe that some children are born with a certain amount of luck from their forefathers. It's almost part of their DNA, and maybe there's some truth to that. *In Norse mythology, **hamingja** (Old Norse "luck") refers to two concepts: the personification of the* *good fortune or luck of an individual or family and is an aspect of the soul or essence of a person.* It's an subset of a person's character and soul under the old mythological teachings. So, some people are born a little luckier or they have great charisma or MOJO, but the moral of the story is that the harder you work, the better you control your emotions, the more you know, and the harder you prepare: THEN, the luckier you probably become. That's just the way it is.

The Spiritual Power of Imagination

By: G Mentz, Esq.

This is a discussion of the imagination with a focus on the teachings of various self help legends such as: Ben Franklin, Marcus Aurelius, Sun Tzu, Emerson, Thoreau, Napoleon Hill, Thomas Troward, James Allen, Wallace Wattles, Norman Vincent Peale, Neville Goddard, and Charles Haanel.

The world is but a canvas to the imagination. ~ HENRY DAVID THOREAU

<u>In the following steps, the beauty and power of the imagination is illuminated. The secrets of how to use imagination as a force for creation and greatness are shown below. Enjoy.</u>

1. We must learn to imagine ourselves in the right state of consciousness, and we must present ideas to our deeper mind and allow our consciousness to accept the ideas.
2. We must learn to think and view the world from a state of consciousness.
3. We must begin to learn how to think from the "finish line", think from the result, or think in the essence of victory
4. Learn to think from a state of mind or a mindset of having and enjoying something
5. We must learn to be in the assumption of having and be able see and feel ourselves "as if" the thing has happened. Think "from" the destiny.
6. In many cases we can think about a desired result or a purpose and look at all of the things that would be true for that result to happen.

7. Imagine looking at a matrix or a mosaic of successful outcomes that would need to happen for the ideal or desire to be manifested.
8. Remember that determined imagination or thinking from the "endgame or result" is the beginning of all great manifestation.

Imagination is the true magic carpet. ~ NORMAN VINCENT PEALE

9. We must imagine ourselves in the feeling of the result fulfilled during our waking hours and before bedtime.
10. We must create a dominant stream of thoughts which would be necessary to be that thing, be the energy of the desire, or to have that thing.
11. This quality of imagination would give us the state of mind or the superior mindset of being into with the purpose or the desired result
12. We can translate imagination and vision into being and becoming.
13. Thinking from the place of purpose is an intense perception of the world of fulfilled desire.
14. Thinking from a standpoint of the desired outcome is creative living.
15. We must put the past into our history and allow our present thoughts to manifest a state of mind which have become a future reality.
16. We have a purpose or find a purpose or seek a purpose we begin to cultivate the necessary hunger in relation to that purpose. That hunger will help continually cultivate the dominant thoughts and the state of mind and the mindset necessary to manifest a greater imagination and results.
17. An imagination is not just limited to the senses of taste, feel, smell, sound or site. Imagination is something where you can close your eyes and see something that you would enjoy in your life and look at it and see the essence of it.

"Imagination should be used, not to escape reality, but to create it."
~ Colin Wilson

18.   For example, if you wanted to be a professional tennis player or a professional pianist, you would see the essence of that result, see yourself performing with crowds, see yourself winning championships, seeing yourself making execution of points or the excellent execution of musical abilities. Seeing yourself victoriously being paid, the type of compensation that is required for a professional.

19.   At some point, you will be able to master a state of consciousness where your dominant thoughts generally pertain towards the results that you desire. Those dominant thoughts would focus on sending you toward the direction of your goals.

20.   This brings us to the idea that your dominant thoughts basically consist of your inner self talk and how you talk to yourself, and the visions, the patterns of the ideas that you see flowing through your consciousness.

21.   If you can seize control over your mind and your memory and directed in a constructive way towards what you want, then you have effectively seized control of your dominant thinking.

Everything you can imagine is real.~ PABLO PICASSO

22.   The real key is to align your mind and your memory and align your inner character and your goals with each other.

23.   Accordingly, when great people say you have to "become that thing" that you want, that means aligning your energy, aligning your vibration, aligning your thinking, & aligning your skills in your mind with that result that you seek.

24.   As such, when the inner and outer worlds match each other is how reality is created.

25.	Some teachers talk about using a trance state or a hypnotic state to push imagination and ideas into the deeper consciousness. The ancient shamans called it Utiseta or "sitting out" which is an exercise where you are able to be in a " clear and peaceful state of mind" with no distractions and you are able to concentrate your mind on things that you want so as to use your imagination in a very vital and constructive way.

26.	When your imagination is so vivid and vital that it becomes real to you. You could sense it. You could touch it. You can do exercises with yourself where you see yourself in a particular situation where you can physically and mentally and emotionally feel the joy of that thing or that essence of being who you want to become. The idea is using your imagination to be, do and have what you want.

"Live out of your imagination, not your history." ~ Stephen R. Covey

27.	Generally some experts talk about how you must become fascinated or intrigued with what you really want. Using your imagination to see and feel happy about something you love. Something that you want to become dedicated and committed to.

28.	It's something that you think about happily and you look forward to. It is the harmonious and positive imagination regarding "what you want" that binds you to it. It creates a pleasant binding effect every time you imagine something with positive feeling,

29.	You are binding, imagining and aligning yourself with what you desire.

30.	The key with aligning yourself is so that your mind is not divided. They always say you don't want a divided house. Similarly, we don't want a divided mind neither. You want your mind, both sides of your mind and your heart and your soul cooperating with each other.

31.	To unify your mental house, sometimes that requires you to weed out the garden as they say and remove some of the anger or the resentment or the prideful emotions that you may have that are connected to something and allow those things to be purged and let go of your mind.

32.   You purify yourself so you can have a more clear and emptier space in your heart in your mind to allow for your imagination to grow effectively and to become aligned with who and what you want to be and what you want to have be and do.

33.   While all desires and results require action, the action begins in your mind and your imagination. There are many great Olympic sportsman or warriors with the military who rehearse every particular event in their mission plans and make sure they understand each task or point from beginning to end. They rehearse what needs to be done in their imagination. Also with this mental and physical practice, it helps winners get in the mindset of being aligned with and receptive to what they want to have.

"The best use of imagination is creativity." ~ Deepak Chopra

34.   You have to center your imagination in the fulfilled desire with complete awareness and sensitiveness. This imagination can initiate optimal rewiring of neural pathways of your inner world.

35.   Sometimes to begin something new and to begin something great, we must allow the old self to die out. The old personality or the old habits can be put aside so we can change our worldview, change our attitudes, change our habits, and change our heart.

36.   We can become a new and open person where we can allow our deeper selves to have what we really, really want.

37.   Sometimes this may require us to rewrite or overwrite the past and sometimes it may require us to review our mindset and look at our memory of certain events and purge them.

38.   If it is something that you feel that you were wronged or something that you feel angry resentful about, sometimes you

may be required to take that situation and look at it for what you learned about life or what lessons you learned from that situation

39.	Even in bad experience, every time something has happened negative in our life, there is a seed of power victory. There is a seed of lessons in that we never have to repeat those particular situations again, can avoid problem, and overcome obstacles that most people can't deal with.

40.	To become renewed and seek new greatness, there will be time where we have to allow ourselves to release old anger, destructive habits, or release resentment because we want to be able to purge the mental garbage.

41.	If we can't forgive, we may need to just let the rubbish go so we can move on.

The man who has no imagination has no wings. ~ MUHAMMAD ALI

42.	We do not want to waste time and be at war with ourselves and nobody wants unnecessarily relive past events in our minds.

43.	We need to remember that the quality of our "frame of mind" and the purity of your mindset is extremely important.

44.	Achieving optimal mind sometimes requires us to forgive and forget but mainly to quit wasting time harping on things, to quit revisiting events in our mind.

45.	Sometimes it's easier to fill the mind rather than just empty it. I remember a great class many years ago where a teach had dirty water in a glass bowl. He then took a hose and started pouring clean water into the dirty bowl of water and it was overflowing at the top. After about five minutes the water was clear in the bowl.

46.	So the point is, is there is two ways to renew and cleanse the consciousness. There is <u>emptying</u> and then there is <u>filling</u>. The key to this exercise is that filling yourself with things that are exciting makes you feel alive and filling your mind with ideas and events you are interested in and are fascinated with changes our attitudes and beliefs.

47.   By that active filling you are releasing and purging, overwriting and pushing out the types of messages and patterns and habits of thinking that are not useful to you.

48.   The Key point here is working to control your dominant self talk. If you increase dominant self talk in a certain area that are constructive and positive and uplifting, at some point your mind or your mindset or your vibration will become persuaded. It will be changed. It will be improved but it will be persuaded with new types of beliefs that will have overwritten the mental state or even the neurons that fire in your brain. They will fire differently after they are trained to fire in certain ways with regard to what you are more interested in and what you are you are more passionate about.

"The possible's slow fuse is lit by the imagination." ~ Emily Dickinson

49.   Over time your inner speech, that dominant speech, that pattern over time will be like a new weaving a certain type of threads into a garment. Over time the garment becomes what you are thinking about. More and more over time, the garment looks like the new types of thoughts and the types of habits and thinking that you have woven into the fabric of your life.

50.   So again in your thinking, we need to observe our inner speech, observe our dominant thoughts and observe those patterns. Because the thoughts that we have, if we pick certain thoughts and certain symbols and certain images in our imagination, we begin to attach certain symbols and certain words and certain ideas to what we want.

51.   So we are attaching our inner ideas and binding them towards our vision and our purpose to augment our worldview and our awareness is what it does.

52.   Remember many times when you change your worldview or you change your attitudes, you expand your awareness in the process. So let's just say for instance you have a new idea

and your new idea is to get a certain type of clothing or a certain type of car, or golf clubs. Your awareness of those new ideas and things becomes heightened. Your awareness of the ideas or dreams that you desire to accomplish is clearer and the path become more reasonable.

53.   When you focus on something, even your awareness of the actual thing becomes heightened. Everybody knows if you buy a certain computer or a certain phone or a certain car, as soon as you have that thing you actually will start noticing others who actually have that type of car. More often you will see that type of car on the street. You will notice your awareness is much higher because you know what that thing is. You understand what that thing is.

"I found I could say things with color and shapes that I couldn't say any other way–things I had no words for." - Georgia O'Keefe, Painter

54.   That's one of the keys with imagination and dominant thoughts along with inner speech. The secret is whatever it is that you want to become, you start to know what that is. You study it, you know what it is on the inside and the outside. You know what the essence or benefits of that thing is. You know what it does. You know how it works. You know the actual dynamics or specs of that thing. That's why again they say to receive something you have to become it or become in alignment with it or match it in energy.

55.   When you know what something is, you recognize it easier. In actuality your mindset needs to be of a harmonious mindset because only those that are harmonious find harmony and they never have to seek for it.

56.   The people that become harmonious attract harmony.

57.   This is just another reason why over the last hundred years, affirmations have become so popular. Prayers and petitions over the last 3000 years have been very popular. Mantras, spiritual poetry, prayers, psalms or repetitious types of readings

where you either read or chant something out loud or in silence have been used for millennia .

58. All these practices of speaking and praying your petitions or incantations are said to help change your mindset, to help change your worldview and it also change your vibration in the way you see things.

59. It can be said that speech is the objectification of the images and the symbols and actions or the reverse of that is images and symbols and actions actually can become your inner speech. They are intertwined backwards and forwards.

"The future belongs to those who believe in the beauty of their dreams." -Eleanor Roosevelt, Politician

60. Remember we need to find our chief aim and purpose. We need to find that desire or goal that we really want and can easily persuade ourselves to accept. Something that we can believe that we are worthy of, something that we can see as our potentiality.

61. Then we need to align with it in both action and speech. Align with our desire, align with our purpose. The right to inner speech is essential.

62. Even if you think about the ancient teachings from the East where they talk about virtuous: speech and mind and awareness. Right speech. Right mind. Right awareness.

63. If you confuse your inner talk in your mind with your outer talk there will be conflict. We need to bring them in alignment with each other and then your actions, tasks, and abilities will manifest much more quickly toward our potential.

64. Generally speaking we are in control of our thought and we are the cause of our inner mental discussion.

65. Now if we seek inspiration, that is a different process of seeking ideas and a stream of thought from the Universe, but your typical daily self talk is another thing. If you activate your inner receptivity, innovative thoughts can come from the

universe. Like Edison and Einstein, both would take naps or rest to seek out solutions to problems.

66.   So alignment is key but what is also vital is cultivating gratitude and feeling. It is powerful to feel grateful for what is going on in your life now. Becoming thankful for your actions and your thinking now.

67.   Choose positive thoughts in relation to what you want.

68.   We have to assume the essence of being what we want to be. I mentioned that once before and I will mention it again that we have to assume the essence.   Here is an example of Essence: So if you want to complete a marathon, you have to see yourself going through it. See yourself going through every part of that race with all the different turns and twists and knowing how much time there will be left at a certain point. Then at the end of the marathon, see yourself completing it and finishing the achievement in a healthy and happy way is your ESSENCE.

69.   You can learn to pre-feel the "essence of being" a winner and essence of being a finisher of that particular event for example.

70.   Review and remember your actions. Reflect in your imagination on what you have done well each day and things you may not have excelled upon. Be determined to be better and do the right thing. Over 200 years ago, Ben Franklin worked his "precepts of order" each evening. He wanted to be excellent and build his character even at a mature age. Practice imagining yourself doing something with excellence and being your best to your loved ones, in your work, or even imagine excellence with your creative or competitive future events.

71.   Considering all of this, every thought that we have, every action that we have, every omission that we have, those things we have in the now are creating our now-ness but they are also weaving our future.

72.   Create your inner speech in a way that blesses your life and others. Your inner speech should bless your health, happiness, love and prosperity.

Perhaps the real trouble was our almost total inability to point imagination toward the right objectives. Twelve Steps and Twelve Traditions, Bill W., Step Eleven, p.100

73.	This may sound oversimplified but we have to make our inner speech blessed and create a flow of good information and good reports. By choosing good things to focus on, this focus forms and inner sense of gratitude, of grateful sense of self talk.

74.	Thus, a Habitual or Habit of consciousness directed upon what we want with a vivid imagination pertaining to it, this clarifies and codifies our energy to manifest our desires.

75.	So with each goal we have a choice and when we make that choice we have to decide whether or not we are going to accept it. When we accept something, it can become a belief or an assumed future belief.

76.	So we are at a point where we are learning to fill ourselves, fill our hearts with the correct information, vibrations, and energy. Fill our minds with dominant ideas and dominant thoughts and dominant speech or inner self talk related to harmony, quality of life that we want.

77.	We need to allow the excellent seed to flourish in our mental garden, and allow the bad seed of the garden really to wither, to be "pushed out" or to die out on its own. All of the unneeded ideas can be overcome with new and powerful ideas that are so strong that the constructive thought will push out from your mind what it is that is holding you back.

78.	In the end, we learn to accomplish these exercises of mind and memory, self talk, and actions/omissions. When all of these things become aligned with each other towards the goals that we want to achieve success can blossom. Our alignment will be towards the happiness we want our lives, towards the health we want in our lives.

79.   Most importantly, we need to identify with the new consciousness. We need to identify with that gratifying consciousness of what we want to be.

80.   So you have to identify with the consciousness of prosperity, love, and harmony. Identify with the consciousness of health. Identify with the consciousness of wealth. All of these things are your consciousness including happiness, health, wealth, worthiness, peace of mind, love. All of these qualities are the most important attributes for bliss and a magnificent recipe for success.

81.   Remember you have to give yourself consent to allow a new mindset to build within your subconscious mind.

82.   I think that's one of the most challenging things about changing attitudes, changing mindset, changing the way we act is one obstacle.   This one obstacle is putting aside wishful-hope and allowing for ourselves to actually and finally change our deeply held beliefs.

83.   We have to give ourselves consent, a mental consent and accept aspiration and authentic change.

"Anything you may hold firmly in your imagination can be yours."
"Our view of the world is truly shaped by what we decide to hear." ~ William James "Father of American Psyciology"

84.   I truly believe that all of these concepts herein form the basis of "liberation spirituality" because you don't have to depend on anybody else for anything. When you become in alignment with yourself and the universe, people, places and things will begin to act in accordance with your harmonious goals. Goals that don't hurt anybody but goals that would help you and other people. Help you serve humanity in a greater way. This is what I mean by liberation spirituality. Each individual could become a greater person and exercise their talents and serve humanity with helping others with the

solutions they may need in their life or becoming the best you can be on a competitive level too.

85.	So to rehash, it is important to learn how to shut out all non productive ideas and divisive seeds in our minds. Shut those things out that interfere with our vision and our purpose and our goals.

86.	Learn to adjust our beliefs and put them at the forefront of our thinking in alignment with our desires and our purpose so as to activate the manifestation of the results what we seek.

87.	To do these things we would fuse ourselves with our purpose and become at one with our purpose. Just like an actor gets into the role and mind of the character.

88.	You could have many purposes. You should make yourself strong and great first for the benefit of yourself and all loved ones.

89.	Your purpose may be helping other people find their path. It could be helping someone become physically healthy. It could be helping someone learn something because you are a teacher or an instructor. It could be any one of those things.

Active imagination requires a state of reverie, half-way between sleep and waking. Without this playing with fantasy no creative work has ever yet come to birth. The debt we owe to the play of the imagination is incalculable. ~ Carl Jung - "Father of Modern Analytical Psychology"

90.	So we have to learn how to choose our state of being, choose our state of consciousness and imagine the receipt of your GOOD on a daily basis. Imagine ourselves in receipt of the essence and benefits of our desires. We have to learn to think from that place of joy and aliveness. Thing from the standpoint of having what we desire. Think from a place of what we will be able to be, have or do. It is only the ideals from which you think that our lives are realized. Your thought creates opportunity, a mindset, and a consciousness.

91.   In this new consciousness, you will have heightened abilities of: awareness, mindfulness, productivity, effectiveness, thought, speech and clarity.

92.   If you are having trouble at any time changing your mindset or breaking out of a mindset that you are stuck in, you need to find a thought or memory that you have that brightened your mood. Something from the past that you can latch onto mentally. Your victorious scene or your "peaceful scene" or your "successful scene" that you can picture in your imagination. You can train yourself to go back to that scene and imagine it "at will", and that will give you peace. With that piece of mind you are able to refocus and re-concentrate and what it is you want.

Conclusion

Remember this isn't about having perfect consciousness or having a perfect mindset that is directed towards your goal. It's really about getting your mindset over 50% clear and productive. Once you have a PMV positive mental vibration of over 50% most all of the time, you will be ahead of the vast majority of all people. You can now have a clear mental vibration of success, health, wealth, wholeness, worthiness, receptiveness, and aliveness. Once you allow yourself to get above 50%, the rewired consciousness takes over. The constructive mindset takes over as 51% of anything is greater than the rest and will color all else in it's vicinity. It's a majority and it takes over the entire mindset and that's the key.

The Power of "It Works"

In this small section, we will divulge some of the greatest secrets to wealth and success ever known. Many people wonder why two people can be given the same recipe for happiness and one gets rich and the other fails. By reading this booklet, you will be provided the power to follow your destiny. You will also be given the steps to success and the missing secrets to happiness that are utilized by the chosen few.

Results Will Prove You Right – Analyze, Diagnose and Clarify

We are herein focused on results and results ONLY. If the system works, then there is no refuting its POWER.

Half measures will avail you nothing. You must not be a wishful person but rather a focused person filled with belief. Rather than sitting around thinking about what you would do if you won the lottery, maybe there is another way. Maybe the people that are relatively wealthy and happy are doing something different to achieve these coveted results?

Would you like a change? Do you want improvement? Are you willing to train your mind to new successful habits and character?

If you are ready, then there is a science to success and a clear and concise path to wealth, health and prosperity.

All of us are using only a FRACTION of our abilities. Each one of us is a powerhouse of energy, consciousness, ideas and action.

From Pythagoras to Plato, from Spinoza to Hegel, and from Schopenhauer to Einstein, the great thinkers of all time imply the same thing. They claim that there are unseen cosmic forces that we can tap into that can energize and guide us to ideas, inventions, power and greatness.

Many of us want things but have we really been sincere? To achieve, we must be truly earnest about our goals. We must have that burning desire, which is something that you will go after and NEVER look back. This is a feeling of authentic PURPOSE where you will dedicate your whole heart to your betterment and becoming your best.

To make this big advancement, you must be willing to let go of your preconceptions. Give up your old ways and become open to a new path, new power and new abundance. What would you do if you could not fail? Truly ask yourself and petition your subconscious for inspiration and guidance. Ask for ideas, ask for help and ask for some sign that will lead you to new heights.

If you are willing to make this quantum leap, get out of your comfort zone and then learn a guaranteed method to riches and success if you are willing to put it to use with PERSISTENCE.

The Master Key List – The Plan

Begin your new life today. Write out 5, 10 or even 50 things that you want to do to improve your life and circumstances. Don't be shy! Write the amazing and exciting things you will achieve about money, travel, relationships, health or whatever. Do it and do it today. As the great poet von Goethe once implied, Begin it TODAY and there is MAGIC and POWER in it.

Write out your Master Key List and put it in your pocket. Think about it for a day. Then pick the 3 most important things you can do to change your life for the better and begin immediately to commit to those 3 goals.

Every day, when you are in your Alpha Relaxed State, you can read the list to yourself. Read it at night and upon awakening. Think about the completed successes. Think about the ESSENCE of your purpose and how you can help yourself, your family and others by attaining your dreams.

As part of your continual growth, you can enhance, add, expand and remove things from your Master Key List.

A Mental Agreement for Specific Success

Your plans and mental blueprint should be very specific. For example, you can write out on a piece of paper a personal commitment to yourself:

> *I, Joe Kahn, Jr., will have a million dollar business 5 years from today. I will sell super creative solutions. I will provide the best service and value to my customers. My products and services will have outstanding benefits for everyone. I will do my best, work hard and remain persistent. I will not falter. Everybody will be happy to pay me handsomely for my services because they will feel great benefits from what I/we provide. I will gladly accept compensation and I will do what is needed to capture and utilize the funds.*
>
> *Sincerely, Joe K, August 2014*

Exercise: If we invoke the INNER POWER/SELF and EARNESTLY ask for [help, harmony and cooperation] , we are drawing closer to the Source. If we can meet the Source halfway, stay tuned into the POWER, and cooperate with the Life Force, our advancement will be speedy.

Exercise: Take some deep breaths ... You mental vibration is important. Can you take time to energize the way you feel about your goal? ... Think about a result that you want. Feel the joy of seeing it. Sense it. Emotionalize it. See your desired result in your mind's eye. Visualize it. Think As If it is YOURS. Think grateful thoughts for the imagined result or something better being manifested in your life. Send the wonderful loving thoughts into the world with heartfelt gratitude and knowing that the universe will bless you on your journey.

Definiteness of Purpose - Knowing what you want and dedicating yourself to it.

Be definite about your desires. On your list:

1. Specify what the desire is. Examples: to weigh the same amount as you did when you graduated from high school, run a marathon, get a promotion, or obtain a better home.

2. Identify exactly what you will do to achieve it.

3. Specify precisely when you will achieve it.

4. Determine what it will feel like to have it and what it will look like.

5. Imagine how you will use your success and envision what emotions you will have when you attain or use your desired outcome.

6. Take some concrete action to move toward your success each and every day.

If the desire is money, then specify the amount, what you will give in exchange for the money and how you will use or invest the money.

While you are building yourself up, associate with those who know about success. Ask encouraging people who know about what you want for help. Many will be happy to give you advice. Model yourself after the best and focus on the best as your belief system will certainly change for the better. Continue to use praise and appreciation in your life as this act of blessing all people and things expands your goodness and brings prosperity and appreciation to you.

When you accomplish any little thing toward your happiness, recognize the goodness of the universe. Be grateful for every small achievement and bless each and every good event that comes your way. Gratitude dispels doubt, keeps you connected, and prevents dissatisfaction. Continue to fix your attention on health, love, success, and good fortune. Your faith will be renewed.

Sincere and heartfelt thankfulness will create a newfound faith in your abilities and allow you to be connected to the great POWER within you.

Initiate Action - Using The Secret Methodology - Tips To Ensure Success.

1. When you want something badly, be sure to allow the universe to bestow upon you the thing you want or something better. Do NOT limit the universe with your desires as the supernatural power may want to give you even more than you seek in new and untold ways.

2. Pray and meditate only for good to happen to yourself and others and avoid negative thoughts or feelings for others or over any situation.

3. See the benefits and purpose of your desire and understand how your desire can help you, all involved, and even assist greater humanity.

4. Seize control of your Charisma and learn to direct and master your Personal Magnetism.

5. Focus on being creative and not just competitive. You can win with your goals and desires by creating new opportunities for yourself and all people.

6. Try to maintain harmlessness in your actions, speech and thinking.

7. Maintain personal responsibility for your actions and take care of your spiritual condition.

8. Give without the expectation of receiving and donate your time and talent to organizations that divinely inspire you and lift up your consciousness.

9. Give your attention to pressing needs first and then when you are stronger as a person, you can go for bigger and bigger goals.

10.   Learn all you can to make yourself ready and capable to achieve any of your stated desires. But remember to take action toward your goals NOW. Taking action can be reading a book, taking a course, calling somebody for an appointment or applying for a position.

11.   Keep your consciousness and mental attitude clear and efficient. If you have done harm to others, try to make it right and continuously maintain your wellbeing by maximizing the excellence of your character by practicing attunement and atonement.

12.   Make a decision. Without commitment and making something important, the ideal will only be a hopeful wish. Your job is to go to the next level and make your move to achieve what you want with all your heart and desire.

13.   Affirm your destiny. Speak it aloud to yourself every day. Say your positive affirmations and prayers out loud in the present tense with feeling and emotion. Speak constructively and learn to speak in an optimistic and confident way.

Remember, one of the greatest abilities of mankind is to give love. We live for the advancement of body, mind and soul and there is no reason to limit our capacities. Many ignorant people see wealth as greed. Ironically, poverty can and will frustrate your relationships with the spirit, other people and those you love. Accordingly, giving is one of the highest forms of love. Give yourself everything you need to become an asset to your community and to the world where one day you may give back as much as you can in great measure.

The Steps to Success – Moving Toward Your Destiny

1. Remember that growth, prosperity and the ability to innovate, create and adapt is your birthright. You are born to be prosperous and excellent.
2. Desire is a power seeking expression. You cannot desire what is not potentially within you; and therefore, you can be what you want to be.
3. Desire is the result of feeling, and the feeling that results from a burning desire is a supernatural faculty seeking and demanding greater expression.
4. Use your free time to hone your skills, improve your knowledge and prepare for your dreams and goals. Do not wait for the perfect opportunity to be all that you want to be. Become all that you can be today, and when an opportunity to be more is offered to you, be ready to take it.
5. Use your place or present business and environment as the means to get a better one. Spend nights and weekends cultivating your abilities and preparing for greater things and the fulfillment of your goals.
6. Everything that touches your life is an opportunity if you discover its proper use. Be aware of each circumstance and study them all for they are your opportunities. Most men fail by hoping for some particular kind of luck, instead of being ready to seize opportunities.
7. Steadily hold the picture of all that you want to attain in person, property and environment. Form a clear conception of it. Then understand that in so far as your desires are not contrary to Eternal Justice, it is absolutely certain that you can be what you want to be. Dwell upon your goal and ideal until it is clear and definite to you and hold it until it arouses intense desire.
8. Your vision of the right idea, if held with faith and purpose, will cause the Supreme Intelligence to move the right opportunity toward you. Then your action, if performed with effectiveness and efficiency, will cause you to move toward the success.
9. Pray with unfaltering grateful faith to the Supreme Intelligence that your desires shall come to you and be

thankful in every prayer, petition or affirmation. Express thanksgiving with a heart full of gratitude that your desires are coming to you.

10. Think about this ideal picture until you are always conscious of it and become in conscious possession of it with positive emotion. Presume it is yours mentally.

11. Desire for everybody what you want for yourself. Be sure to take nothing from anybody without giving a full equivalent in life and value; the more you give, the better for you.

12. Use each day to the fullest and do each act efficiently and effectively without haste. You must put the expanding thought into everything you do and communicate excellence to all whom you deal with.

13. Know that others from around the world desire to help you now that you are on the supernatural path. You are to cooperate and be willing to receive this mutually beneficial exchange and assistance from those who are sent to you.

14. The basic element of success is therefore to hold the thought and the mental attitude of advancement and to be excellent in all that you do.

15. Strive to maintain a Consciousness of your being at one with the Spiritual Power of the Universe. Know that you are connected to the Creative Power and begin now to co-create your destiny. Utilize these steps in all of your affairs.

Conclusion:

Gratitude and Thankfulness lead to greater constructive expectation in our daily living. Positive expectation, belief and confident expectation are FAITH. Repudiate miracles and you will receive NONE. Recognize possibility and IT WILL APPEAR. Praise others, bless others and bless and Praise YOURSELF. Blended with Humility, your harmonious connection to the universal spirit and supply will allow a pipeline of grace upon you. Remain teachable and keep a Thankful Heart as gratitude is HIGHLY conducive to Faith, Confident Expectation and Living with JOY. Know forgiveness in your heart. Feel and know that the world forgives you. Realize that you can now forgive all transgressions once and for all. With your forgiveness, you free your mind's mental and spiritual power. What you think about is EXPANSIVE in your LIFE. Your focus on the good and the great will bring the good and the great into your awareness and into your world.

Be contemplative (consciously thinking) while in action as this is the key. Having a focused and harmonious connection to your deeper intelligence while working effectively toward your ideals will continually reveal results. You are part of all possibilities. Seize upon your divine rights to supply and success. Allow yourself to be great and to do great things. There is no need to compete. YOU MUST CREATE. Create new ways of doing things, provide quality service, create solutions, provide opportunity and help others. Follow your true place toward your dreams and your talents will be revealed. If you exercise the practical steps of gratitude, faith, visualization, meditation/prayer and action, the sixth sense will emerge and you will know when to take action on ideas and how to fulfill them to completion.

Be patient and live harmoniously in a state of gratitude. The picturing and presumption of your success coupled with action, feeling, love and faith will lead to great things. Ask and you shall receive and be ready to receive what you desire. You may have challenges or even be dealt a blow of rejection; however, the universal force allows the best outcomes. You may not get exactly what you want, but something better may be available for your receipt and cultivation soon thereafter. In your journey, you will be protected from bad situations and afforded the opportunities for even better ones.

The Law of Achievement was first delivered as a lecture, and part of this famous guidance was given in China, Arabia, Europe, India, Latin America, The West Indies, and through Asia. Here is the framework for success that has been proven over the last 25 years.

I. Ideas and Belief

TAKE CONTROL OF YOUR MIND - All creation and goals begin with an idea. Our belief system about ideas and goals must be based on the probability of reasonably good results.

II. Definitiveness of Purpose

Focus your heart and actions upon a definite, well developed purpose as a life-dedication.

III. Acceptance

We must believe that prosperity and well-being are our birthright. Believe that the possibility of abundance and riches is a reasonable option for your purpose and commitments. When your dominant thoughts revolve around your Purpose, your overriding mental energy will be a catalyst to the manifestation of what you desire. When firm belief, earnestness and constructive emotion are in back of a burning desire, the purpose is energized. We must understand the rationale behind our desires. The who, what, when, where and why we must achieve the outcome and how it will help are all involved.

IV. Self-Regard, Worthiness and Confidence

SELF-REGARD - With opportunity comes responsibility toward your mental, physical and spiritual health. Do what works to take care of yourself with diet, exercise, learning, sleep and fellowship. Prune habits that stand in the way of your happiness and health. This practice will instill a power of worthiness. Ask for help if need be.

FEED YOURSELF with food, news and information that can make you highly skilled, happy, successful, and healthy. Develop great routines and habits. Become excellent, simplify your life, empty the clutter and refine your focus.

V. Clarity and Focused Energy

MENTAL ATTUNEMENT - Before implementing each plan or taking any big step, we evaluate our mental effectiveness. Getting clear and going through a mental catharsis will free our thinking abilities. This means to look at your track record, atone, prune, purge and clear away the mental debris. Begin to master "what works best for you" and start to utilize the practices that make you efficient and healthy.

VI. Invest in Yourself and Prepare for the Future

HABIT OF INVESTING IN YOUR EXCELLENCE – Spend time and money WHEN it is an investment in yourself, your future, your business, your retirement, your education and travel, your loved ones or risk management tactics.

VII. Right Livelihood and Labor of Love

PASSION - Occupational analysis can turn work into play. Research ideas - what are your passions, how do your ideas serve? Create plans, look at what it would take to be successful, then act on them, implement your strategies, review and improve them each year.

VIII. Action and Boldness

Having a clear mind that is working creatively allows for big choices where commitments may be selected. Commitment creates a nucleus of new momentum and begins a chain reaction of creation. Each day will become an opportunity to move closer to achievement by doing each act or task in an efficient and effective manner. Do it right the first time and you will not need to do it again.

IX. Imagination and Visualization

Using the mind to picture and emotionalize your success is one of the golden keys to prosperity and success. This allows you to see your future or pre-dream your destiny. You can effectively build what you want in your mind. This act of mental preparation can save years of time as a shortcut toward your ultimate successes. See yourself in optimal circumstances in your mind's eye and FEEL it. If you can visualize the optimal result, then see the next step. Example: see yourself a few pounds leaner toward your optimal weight.

X. Character Development

CHARACTER - Thinking or what is thought about habitually becomes who you are. The totality of your thought and action is your character. Radiate excellence, cheer and zeal. Build yourself from the inside out, do each act with effectiveness, and others will see your great character and dedication to excellence. Make wealth and excellence a priority. Align your thoughts with success, health and prosperity.

XI. Enthusiasm

Enthusiasm will enable you to "saturate" all with whom you come in contact with interest in you and in your ideas. It is the foundation of a Pleasing Personality, and you must have such a personality to influence others to cooperate with you. When belief, earnestness and constructive emotion are in back of a purpose, it is energized and increases the probabilities of success and even luck. Be teachable, learn to receive from others, offer praise and appreciate life.

XII. Discipline

SELF-CONTROL is an engine that can steer you into great opportunities and away from problems. Determine who you want to associate with, who you want to have relationships with and who you want to do business with. Keep lists and do three constructive things per day toward the fulfillment of your dreams to the best of your ability.

XIII. The Law of Increase

When you provide service or products to others, you should convey the energy of increase to all. In this way, people know that when you are providing help, their lives and abilities are increasing. You are providing solutions to problems and easing the suffering of others by your service. Further, we must comprehend ways in which how our ideas and success will help others.

XIV. A Constructive Attitude

Cultivate a pleasing and confident personality. Develop affirmations that assist in lifting your vibration to higher levels where you are perceived as somebody that others would want to help and cooperate with. Example: "I am energetic, creative, whole, healthy and wealthy. I am rich with life and love." Become a beacon of abundance and excellence. Learn to think and speak in prosperous ways that conveys confidence, opportunity and cheer. Mold the habits and tendencies of your thought toward an attitude of well-being and optimism.

XV. Organized Thought

Having the power to direct your thinking will ultimately create your reality. Knowing the facts affects your ideas and actions. Do your best to have the most factual inputs and your outputs will be more accurate.   What is thought about habitually becomes who you are and affects what you do, how you act, what you receive and what you achieve. Think, feel and act "AS IF" you are in possession of what you want to obtain. Cultivate emotions and your character around the "AS IF."

XVI. Contemplation and Quantum Leaps

MEDITATIONS AND PRAYER - Write out affirmative meditations such as "Each day I am improving". Write out 10 statements that are affirming and positive. Contemplate over them each day. Ask for inspiration from your subconscious or from your divine connection. Seek to expand your life. Go past your comfort zones. List goals beyond your expectations and have specific deadlines. You can always change the dates.

XVII. Monitoring and Inventory

Every outcome contains a lesson that is the seed of future success. Even if you fail, you learn invaluable lessons that may guide you to greater and greater heights. Study your days, reflect on your activities. Decide how to continually improve yourself. Do your homework and do all you can to learn and know your niche. Look at where you are, who you are and where you are going.

Then you can periodically reset your course and navigate to optimize the journey. Devote 20 percent of your waking hours each week to your passion. If you become great at it, odds are you can also earn a living doing it.

XVIII. Harmlessness

Treat others in a way that you would treat yourself. Help others make the best of themselves. Teach others these steps and you will be able to help them live to their highest order. As they say, we must give it away to keep it. Learn to focus your days on constructive activities and avoid senseless arguments with those who do not care about your success.

XIX. The Third Force – Networking and Support Groups

GROUP OR NETWORK - This concept is timeless in that if two or more people are gathered, a third force of energy and creativity presents itself. Model yourself after successful people. Do what the winners do. Ask successful people for advice or insights. Join a local business group. You must carefully select those whom you ask to be part of your business network. Make sure they have specialized knowledge, a good track record and are supportive and encouraging.

XX. Develop your Intuition and Sixth Sense

Learn and practice awareness, keep a journal, write out creative thoughts, develop and allow a universal flow of ideas into your mind. Continue to work all of these steps in all of your affairs while maintaining your purpose and dedication and while helping others who want prosperity and peace of mind.

25 Mental Exercises to Augment Consciousness

1. The first exercise is to experience feeling the extensions of your body. For example, try to sense your toes. Try to feel each toe. Move each toe and feel the sensation of each movement. The key to this exercise is to mentally sense that part of the body in exclusion to all others.

2. Here is an eye exercise. Upon awakening while in your bed, use these simple eye exercises. First, move your eyes left to right (5 times). Next move your eyes up and down five times. Then, move your eyes in a circle five times either clockwise or counterclockwise. Finally, move your eyes diagonally from the top right to bottom left or top left the bottom right (five times) These exercises will help stimulate the brain, consciousness and sensory awareness.

3. The next exercise is to breathe while listening. As you inhale, try to listen to your inhalation. If you close your eyes during the exercise, you can focus on the air moving in and out. Trying to notice your breathing muscles and the sounds to the exclusion of all other sensations. This exercise can help you realize the power of your breath, the power of your lungs, and the importance of the element of the air.

4. Here is an energy exercise -   Some people refer to this exercise as an ancient type of yoga. With your hand or finger, close one nostril and take a deep breath through your other nostril, hold it for a few seconds, and then exhale for your mouth. Switch sides and take a breath for the other nostril hold it, and exhale from your mouth. This alternating nostril and breath exercise can invigorate your interior breathing areas. As you might guess many people only breath through one nostril the majority of the day, and thus, this exercise can stimulate underused areas of the nasal passages, lungs, and brain.

5. **Sending healing currents.** This exercise is a method of sending healing energy from your consciousness into the organs of your body more to your extremities. Relax your body from head to toe, then imagine healing currents in your brain within our mind.

You can imagine this energy as a white color. Imagine sending those healing energy currents from the top of your brain near your eyes, moving to the back of your brain, moving down to your spine through your neck, and into your body. Imagine sending these healing currents to any part of your body that has discomfort or that needs to be energized

6. **White noise exercise** - Sometimes a static sound or background noise can stimulate a mental activity. Most of us have been on a plane, or been driven down the highway, or have ridden on a bus where there's plenty of engine noise. While resting during the ride, we have pleasant thought and interesting ideas and sometimes amazing creativity is stimulated. During this time, close your eyes if you can and listen for ideas & listen for inspiration. Music to a song, words to a book or even important tasks or solutions to problems can come to us during this period of introspection.

7. **Here's an associational exercise**. Take an image or idea. Next, search your mind and memory for what that image or idea brings up in your mind. This exercise is an amazing process and taps of your mind to see the information that you retain. Try and go deeper and find what ideas, people or places that come to mind.

8. When you recall ideas or memories, do you see images what do you see words or do you actually hear something. Some people's memories operate in different ways. Some people sense: sounds, emotions, images, feelings, smells and so forth. In your imagination, try picking something up and imagine its weight, its texture, and its color. This is just another exercise that will help you improve your sensory perception, memory and your imagination.

9. Try to dictate in something into your phone or into your computer. Try telling a story about something that happened to you or to another person. After you have dictated read what you've said. Evaluate the transcript. Does this voice in the transcript writing look different then how you normally write

ideas. The key to this exercise is that you're writing voice maybe completely different then your authentic dictated voice. Which one do you like better?

10.   **A prayer exercise** – If you pray regularly, try saying a completely original prayer. Try making a prayer that has nothing in it than you've ever said before in a prayer. Do this new prayer sincerely and in earnest. This is just another way for you to express your originality and sincerity with gratitude and mindfulness. This process may expose deeper hopes, desires and beliefs.

11.   **The metaphysics exercise** – Try practicing another philosophical or spiritual path for a few weeks or months. Read some books about a new philosophy or attend a lecture or a different type of religious service. The idea here is to expand and affirm the boundaries of your beliefs philosophy. This is a great exercise to enhance and expand your beliefs almost as an exercise of cultural exchange.

12.   **Imaginary room exercise.** Close your eyes and imagine yourself in a different place or a room that you've either been inside before or never been in before. Walk around the room or place in your minds eye. What do you see, what are the dimensions of the room, what or who is in the room. If someone is in the room, can you have a conversation with them mentally. Can you ask that person questions about your future. This is just an exercise to stimulate your imaginative ability. When you develop this type of imagination, you can use it to formulate plans, ideas and exercise objectives.

13.   **A quick seven direction exercise** – When you awaken or before you are ready to go to bed, stand up and face North. As you are facing North, say softly, I am thankful to the North for this day and every day. Then turn to your right, and thank the East for this day and every day going forward, Then turn to the South, and thank the South for your health and happiness and joy. Then turn to the West, and thank the West for love and aliveness. The, look downward and thank the earth for its

energy, and then look above to the heavens and be thankful for the stars. Then close your eyes and look into your heart and thank the universe for your power. You are now done, and can say, "It is so". After this, open your eyes as this is the conclusion of this gratitude exercise.

14.   **A writing exercise**- Write down five things you want to create in your life. For each of these five things, write down the most important task that is required for these ideas, objectives, or creations to manifest. This process will stimulate the desire to create and inspire the expression of those ideas. This method will also illuminate what is required to manifest your goals.

15.   **Grounding exercise** – Lay down on the floor or in the grass on your back. Take a moment to relax. Try relaxing your body. Begin by relaxing your head, then down to your heart, to the lungs, and down to relax your toes. Next role to your side and rest on your side for a moment. Then roll to your belly. This is an extremely simple exercise to stimulate the body and energize the blood from you back to your side and to the front of your body. The amusing part of this exercise is this. If most people went to a kindergarten playground and played for 5 minutes every day, they would probably be happier, healthier and live longer without illness.

16.   **A perception and exercise** – Look at a scene or look at the room or look outside. Next close your eyes and try and remember every detail that you've just seen. This is a great exercise to expand your perception and awareness. This exercise can instill a greater ability to remember things around you while also helping to deepen and widen your perception during your daily life.

17.   **A listening exercise** –Try to listen distantly. Take a moment and calm your mind. Then, listen to what is happening around you. Try and discern what you hear at a distance. Try to name all the sounds that you hear far away. This exercise can greatly improve your audio awareness and sentience.

18.   **Something new** – Buy or order something new to eat. When you get something new to eat, take your first bite, close your eyes, and breathe gently; then, <u>savor</u> the new flavor. This exercise can enhance your sense of smell, your sense of taste, and your sense of discernment.

19.   **A new route** – one day soon try a new path or new route, or try a new game or buy a new type book. These types of new activities can awaken new parts of your deeper mind. This will also teach you the ability to say yes to something new and interesting. You may also want to practice <u>saying no</u> to something that you don't really want to do. This exercise will allow you to expand your opportunities, and to limit the waste of time in your life.

20.   **Box something exercise** – If you have a pain or memory that you don't like, try to box-in the idea in your mind. If you have a pain in your foot for example, close your eyes and put a metal box around that pain. The idea is to compartmentalize that feeling and "box it in" and prevent the rest of your body from being affected by it. In the same vein, imagine a past event that may be upsetting to you. Box that event in your mind, and imagine that box leaving your mind, and flying away into outer space. While the box floats away, imagine it burning up into flames and being destroyed. The idea of this exercise is to either compartmentalize something to reduce the effect or to "box it" to make it irrelevant. Much like a temporary file on a computer, sometimes files need to be selected and shredded and removed.

21.   **A new person exercise** - The next time you meet someone new, ask them their name. When they tell you their name, try to associate it with someone you've known before with the same name. Or associate the name with an idea or a color. The key to this exercise is to see if you can become better at remembering people or ideas while associating new ideas with other embedded memories or concepts.

22.   **A detoxifying exercise** – In the morning or before going to bed try this breathing technique. Take a breath into the nose and say to yourself "In with gratitude" then hold that breath, then gently exhale from your mouth while thinking are saying to yourself, "out with attitude". This exercise is especially good at bringing in positive energy and releasing negative energy.

23.   **Affirm what is good exercise** – Think of a person place of thing that has been positive in your life. Think of three of five things that you like or appreciate about this person place or thing. This exercise can be extremely powerful in helping your mind affirm constructive and inspirational ideas and memories in your life. This exercise can also create that shift and consciousness to dominant thoughts of positivity.

24.   Get in a quiet place where there are no distractions and think of the alphabet. Think of a letter. Select the letter "J," for instance. Think of a person in your family or in your childhood with a "J" in their name who you were very fond of or even loved. Ponder that loving emotion. Think of the happy times you had with this person. Bless that person in your mind. Consider the ability to transfer this feeling to another person in your current life.

25.   Think of a color, for example, blue. Think of something blue that you owned that gave you happiness in the past. Harvest that emotion. Feel it. Try to re-live the joy of having the thing. Consider one of the five senses (taste, touch, smell, hearing, seeing). Select one, such as smell. Remember your favorite aroma. Think back about the flavor or pleasant smell. Ponder the joys of enjoying that aroma again, for example, a great cup of espresso in Venice, Italy. Experience the moments in the past that you enjoyed in conjunction with the feeling and senses. Allow gratitude to fill the mind, Spirit, and body.

Conclusion

On a more practical level, life and many of the objectives that we will want to achieve will involve a fundamental process. This methodology will usually include an investigation, diagnosis, analysis, benchmarking, planning, action, implementation, monitoring, and continuous improvement. In urgent situations, we will call upon all of what we know to do our best in any emergency, but most of the important issues are long-term ideals where we have time to prepare.   Similar to project management or wealth management practices, these steps are general in nature and involve many sub-tasks and sub-activities. These activities may also relate to the tenets of philosophy such as: Perception, Higher Potential, Efficient Action, Articulation and Speech, Understanding and Listening, Concentration, Gratitude, Effort, Action, Contemplation, and Focus.

Exercise:

Take some deep breaths…. Breath In Life Energy and allow the old energy out with your exhale. Your mental state and vibration is important. Next, can you take time to energize the way you feel about your result/goal…. Think about a higher ideal that you want. Feel the joy of seeing your desired result. Sense it. Emotionalize it. Whether it be health, wealth, relationships or success, observe your desired result in your mind's eye. Think As If it is YOURS. Think grateful thoughts for the imagined improvements or even something better being manifested in your life. Send the wonderful thought out and into the universe with heartfelt gratitude.

Mission Team Success Management

Team Issues to Consider - When you are planning a goal, a long term idea, or you simply have a great objective there are many issues to look at. Here is a check list. You can look at an idea or a challenge or problem, and begin to put a strategy in place to surmount the challenge and follow your dreams. Remember, there is never struggle but only partial success and each unfinished success adds up into winning knowledge, skill, and advancement.

1. **Look at the Challenge and Potential Solution**. Example: Getting Fit for a Competition
2. **Analysis** - Analyze Situation or Goal that can solve the Problem.
3. **Diagnosis** - Diagnose problem, competition, creative goal, or solutions.
4. **Preliminary Intel -** Cultivate data and inputs to create the Mission Plan and itemize its needs.
5. **Planning** - Develop a plan using research and/or experts
6. **What is the Total Purpose of the Mission?** – Defined objectives - What is the Target of the Objective. Success is the Target.
7. **Diagram or Chart the Mission** into Phases or Time Frame
8. **Human Performance** - Engage Team Selection via tactical HR Human Resources. If it is only you, that is OK, but if you need team members or assets, you can recruit or employ them.
9. **Assets** - Leaders and team must be equipped, skilled, and have access to quality information, tools, and data assets.
10. **Execute -ability** - Determine methods of execution of the plan or mission
11. **Comprehension Factor** - Ability to understand and articulate the plan
12. **Task Management** - Prioritize the plans tasks in subsets or increments.

13.   **Contingency Planning** – Knowing what to do if common problems arise.

14.   **Landscape and Typography of the Mission** – Understanding the directions and what you need to have to get from point A to B.

15.   **External Systems used in Battle** – Systems that all parties are using.

16.   **Internal Systems used in Battle.** Computers or Communications that would be used only within the team.

17.   **Communications** - Mandate and itemize communication channels and methods.

18.   **TimeFrame** – Methods to monitor and to Execute or deadlines for each task which coordinate with the rest of the team roles.

19.   **Sustainability** of the team vision, mission and roles.

20.   **Continuous Education** - Education of team is continuous until mission date.

21.   **Culture** - Create a culture of extreme excellence based on stats, results and accuracy of each role.

22.   **No Assumptions** - Incomplete data areas must be filled and sought to be filled incessantly.

23.   **Synergistic** - Team excellence, synergy, and trust and group dynamics.

24.   **Response-Ability** - Ownership of results and the mindset of success.

25.   **Personal/Unit Consciousness** - Healthy body, mind, soul and Ego in tandem with the team or for the individual . Team achievement consciousness.

26.   **Efficiencies** - Simplifying tasks and roles for efficiency with are customized for any goals or mission.

27.   **Hazards and Perils** - Risk analysis is essential to be prepared for anticipated risk and ways to overcome such risk.

28.   **Opponent or Competitive Environment** – Who can hurt you and how? Does the enemy need to be avoided, confronted, or eliminated?

29.   **Decentralized** – Roles spread out with each team member having backup skills to compensate for any weakness created by the accident, elements or enemy.

30.   **Individuation** – Authentic goals with designated roles for yourself or each member of the team.

31.   **Authorizations** - Delegated authority for you or team members.

32.   **Confidence Factor** - Belief in achievement potentiality of mission-goal by leader and team.

33.   **SWOT analysis** of each role and overall goal. Look at Strengths, Weaknesses, Opportunities and Threats.

34.   **Implementation** – How to implement each task by each role member to complete of finish the objective successfully.

35.   **Calculated Execution** - Quick and calculated decisions that are ready to be utilized during the mission or plan.

36.   **Monitor Results** – Continuous Information and Data Extraction CIDE

37.   **Continuous Improvement** - Continually improve team roles, skills, and education while learning from data.

38.   **Incentives** - Systems of incentives and motivation. How to reward yourself or the Team. This can be in writing before the execution begins.

Acronym Exercises:

Here are some exercises of consciousness. These Acronyms are ways to embed ideas into your deeper mind and imagination. Read each one 3 times and try to comprehend each statement with your own conception of what each statement means to you.

1. IC - Instead of "I think, therefore I Am", a Physicist may say, "I see, therefore it is"
2. BU – You must be yourself, and become who you were meant to be. Be Authentic.
3. UR – You must know that your is-ness is your connection to the universe.
4. CU – You must see yourself as you want to BECOME or see what you want to BE, HAVE or DO.
5. IB – I become what I think about all day. My being is based on my I and my identity that is accepted.
6. NU – The imagination and power is within when you are aware of your connection.
7. YU – Why NOT you. Your celestial inheritance is waiting for you. Your deeper consciousness wants to accept the gifts.
8. 6 ¢ - Sixth Sense - Use your inspiration, ideas, imagination, and creative intuition to follow your dreams and manifest your destiny.
9. B4U – You must be "FOR YOU", and mentally a proponent for yourself development, self regard and improvement of your life. Be on your

own team. Be your own cheerleader. Persuade yourself of your potential. Don't be a mental house divided.

10. BC – You will eventually Be what you see on the picture screen of your mind. Creative visualization can be practices and enhanced.

11. URNRG – You are energy. You are pure being. Be aware of your spiritual energetic creative self. Be aligned with what you want in life. Be aware of the signs and symbols of the universe's desire to assist you. Be aware of your gratitude and thankfulness. You can tap into the unlimited supply of the universe with your awareness of the NOW.

12. CN2BU – Seek inside of yourself. It is an inside job. Lean to control your inner dominant thoughts. Look deep within to clear away the past, build yourself up, learn all you can, and take action to be your best so that you may help yourself, your loved ones and humanity.

Keep the Engine Running Smoothly –Attunement and Purification

From time immemorial to the present day, religions and philosophies have urged mental purification. Some organizations have formal rites of purification from baptism to confession and others hold "one on one" spiritual counseling with others to assist them in dissipating the mental patterns and habits which may be holding someone from advancement in their personal and professional life.

One way to help yourself in freeing your mind from obsessions or negative thoughts is to help others. Therefore, if we serve another, we may get out of our problems. The story of the early founders of some spiritual bodies and 12 step programs clearly states that finding another to work with kept them on the right track. Plus, members of groups or spiritual philosophies have a common bond where they better understand each other's lives and past. This process of catharsis and atonement was one of the missing keys to their success with the 12 step program healing and wholeness process. Thus, giving your spirituality to another is an integral part of inner growth and healing others. Listening to another with compassion, humility, and the willingness to help will return spiritual gifts to you in the long run. In any event, this process can also make us conscious of our old pains and reaffirm why we do not want to go back to the merry-go-round of self-will. The wonderful characteristic of service is that service is compassion. Service can heal the giver and receiver just as compassion does.

Forgiveness, Willingness and Amends

There will come a time where you will have an opportunity to make direct amends to another person for something that you have done wrong. As I don't advise spilling your beans to another person for your own self-satisfaction, you should carefully analyze how you do this and what you will say.   Keep it simple, and say, "I was wrong about the way I acted in the past" or "I want to apologize to you for the things I did" or "I was wrong, and I take responsibility for any hard feelings". Basically, "It was my fault, I was wrong, I accept responsibility, and I am sorry." That's it, that's all, and walk away. Just leave, move on, and you can always try to improve on it from there.

Remember, many of these people just want to get on with their life and deserve respect. So, we should recognize others rights and feelings throughout all of this. As a note, nobody is urging the reader to apologize for a possible petty crime or possible felonious activity in the past, and you should consult with a lawyer or spiritual advisor before taking any large step, but most amends are easy and most normal folks are happy to mend bridges. The important thing is that we do our part.

If you can't meet with the person, you can always write a letter to them. Don't write a confession. Just say you apologize for the past situation, and you can also ask for reconciliation if that is possible. You can always pray for the person that you have harmed. You can pray that they receive peace, happiness, and all the best. Overall, it is you whoe will benefit the most from this action. You can always look at the issue and determine what you learned from it. You will often find that the past confrontation or relationship problem is a "lesson that you will never need to repeat again". Lessons are good and only make us better. Additionally, you can write about the problem or resentment. Write it all out and find where you erred. Then just burn the paper when you are done. Free your mind and don't empower the negative thoughts anymore.

Dwelling and House Divided

It is a waste of our time to continue to dwell on a past hurt. Yes, we need sometimes to air it out and clear away the debris. But, to continue to let it fester and allow a seed of resentment or anger to grow into a mighty weed in the mind is not healthy.

Don't give another person, place, or institution free rent in your head. Evict them with love, prayer, gratitude, amends, turning it over, and making the best of your life. If you remain in a state of bitterness, it can muddy your own water and affect our day to day creativity and efficiency. It can tear down the relationships with family, spouse, and friends. Moreover, a mind full of confusion and anger can block off the spiritual connection with the Supreme. Don't fall prey to this mind game. You now have the strategy to grow out of this. Get up and do something about it.   If you stay messed up for a long time with anger, anxiety, depression, you may need to see a professional or even seek out medical help and medication.

Do this under the care of a physician who can monitor your progress. Possibly see a counselor or analyst while under the care of a physician. Overall, be honest with yourself and don't deny the very help that may change your life. Your life can enter into new growth, creativity, and well being as you work through this process.

Forgiving Self

Never forget that amends includes other people, but it also includes you. We need to forgive ourselves. We need to develop self-respect. We must develop some type of self-love. Accordingly, make amends to yourself. Over time, we should learn to take care of ourselves and have self-respect and self-esteem. This is also where meditation and affirmations can be empowering. Find quotes or create your own affirmations that empower your mind and help rewrite the consciousness with thoughts of freedom, aliveness, success, health, and prosperity.

Attention and energy focus:

We can choose to focus our energy on good or bad. There is a good and supernatural use of our self-will and willingness. Allowing or willing ourselves to think about good, loving, tolerant, and harmless thoughts can create inner power. Willing ourselves to build our self regard, to help others, to be grateful, and to cultivate a spiritual consciousness are paths to power and freedom. It is much like exercise the spiritual muscles. Lets face it, suiting up and doing something is the first action into a routine that can change the focus of your state of mind.

There may be a family member or friend who has attributes that you don't like. Your job may have tasks that you cannot stand. The key to this process is to focus your thoughts and energy on what you do like about a person or situation. What are you thankful for?

It is ridiculous for me to quit on a friend or my job because I do not like 1% of what that relationship entails. It is also a mistake to sabotage my relationships with everybody because I don't like one tiny thing about them. With that being said, if a person has an attribute that goes against the very grain of your existence, you may have to separate yourself from that job or relationship. I am speaking of attributes such as criminal behavior, complete dishonesty, constantly stealing your energy while giving nothing in return, or chronic drug or alcohol use and so on.

Clear Your Mind – Banishing Negativity for Abundance - Attunement

Steps of Attunement. The clearing away of mental debris through a process of self-analysis and attunement will allow us to obtain greater peace of mind and mental effectiveness toward abundance.

1.   Remain Teachable: Keep right-sized with regard to our ego.

2.   Developing Character: Seek change and be open to growth. Eliminate what is not useful and adapt for new abilities

3.   Honesty and Integrity: Do what you say and be honest with yourself.

4.   Purity of Thought: Keep your thinking clear, act in the now, and enjoy each moment.

5.   Be Selfless: Give without expectation of return through service and non-hoarding of things and yourself. Circulate your goodness and radiate your excellence.

6.   Develop Higher Purpose: Making healthy decisions to have a definite purpose toward your objectives or advancement for all.

7.   Appreciation: Be thankful for the gifts you have received, praising others and blessing your home, family, and world.

8.   Reflection: Maintain a willingness to engage self-analysis and evaluation for the purposes of growth.

9.   Attunement: Seek harmony to heal disputes with others through amends, restitution, mental catharsis, character development, and right action.

10.   Visualization: Use contemplation, prayer, or meditation to enable a mental vision of a fuller life and connection to the universe. Apply constructive meaning to present or past events.

11.   Open Mind: Keep the motivation to be open-minded about accepting a state of well-being and peace.

12.   Love and Harmony: Allow peace and tranquility in your life, and embrace a sincere belief that life is abundant and that love and harmony can be allowed into your heart permanently

Skill and Knowledge

I would still have endless disappointment if I continued to desire to be and do things without the necessary understanding of it. If I want to build a wonderful software, then I may need to know how to program it. I may need to know the background about the content that is being used. If I want to be a doctor, I will need to prepare to become admitted to medical school and learn about the requirements and admissions processes. However, if I want to be the best race car driver in the world, I may not need to know how to repair the engine. Do you see what I am saying?

You will require certain specific skills to go toward the desires and dreams that you have. Make sure that you are focused on what you need to know. The best surgeon in the world does not need to know how to build the operating table or equipment; he or she just needs to know how to use it better than anyone. If you are in sales, it helps to understand the product or service. If you understand the product of service, you may develop the necessary belief that the product and service is good for all who use it. You may also learn to explain the advantages of having or using what you are selling. The necessary understanding can come from books, videos, school, or your advisors. The more understanding you have, the more prepared you are to explain, defend, and promote the item. Not only that, you will understand how to assist others with the strategies that you now understand. If you want a direct resource, seek out those who have achieved what you want to achieve. They can speak from personal experience about what you need to do. You may even try to think and act like they do. If you emulate the qualities of the best, you may become the best.

10 Peace & Prosperity Ideas from Great Authors and Self Help Books

Having an annual resolution is not necessary, but I am providing 10 financial independence related ideas for you to consider for your own financial freedom and peace of mind.

1. **Freedom Fund** - Try to save 6 months or a year of income so that you are free to leave a job, take time off, or get through a tough time. **Author Credit:** Brian Tracy

2. **Let Go of Bad Clients** - Get rid of bad customers. Customers that waste everyone's time are not worth it. If you have a great service, you can always raise your prices and provide VIP service to your great customers and earn even more. **Author Credit**: Dr. Richard Carlson

3. **Know the Rules** - Invest in Blue Chip diverse funds or ETFs with a good track record. However, know the rules of the game, and avoid excessive fees.   **Author Credit:** Tony Robbins.

4. **Seek Excellence** - Successful people attract wealth. Focus on being great at what you do. **Author Credit:** Dr. Wayne Dyer

5. **Consciousness** - "Wealth is a state of awareness that allows you to tap into your inner creativity in order to fulfill a need that somebody else has. **Credit**: Dr. Deepak Chopra.

6. **Pay Yourself First** - That means, the first money that comes out of the pot is your savings! **Credit**: Suzy Orman and T Harv Ekar stress this point.

7. **Get Rid of Bad Loans** - Get rid of high interest loans and credit cards, create an emergency cash fund, or work on saving for college for kids. **Author Credit.** Dave Ramsey

8. **Be Yourself** - "Don't get caught up with what other people are doing. Being a contrarian isn't the key but being a crowd follower isn't either. You need to detach yourself emotionally." **Credit**: Warren Buffet

9. **Seize Opportunity** - "Behind me is infinite power. Before me is endless possibility, around me is boundless opportunity. My strength is mental, physical and spiritual." **Credit** – 50 Cent

10.   **Manage Your Risk Management** - "Life insurance is sometimes said to be a horrible investment; but if you are healthy and have 3 children, the premiums seem to be a pretty good deal". **Credit** ~ George Mentz

The 48 Rules of Power – Creating Your Destiny

1.   As beings that desire increasing life, we each contain energies of body, mind and spirit of which we must maintain equilibrium between all three energies. To preserve this balance we utilize our threefold powers. Use of mental, spiritual and physical powers in a methodical and way must produce quantum abundance.

2.   All thoughts begin with an idea which is the byproduct of divine connection to the source of all thought.

3.   The ideas in back of the thought are the mystical form of all creation and the underpinnings of tangible results or manifestation.

4.   All thoughts tend to lead to the field of potential outcomes for all actions, inactions, and creation.

5.   Deep Thinking or what is believed in mind habitually becomes who you are and is your essence or character.

6.   Free will creates Choices where commitments must be selected. We all have the ability to choose how we use free will in terms of thoughts and actions.

7.   Choices create the nucleus of new form and begin a chain reaction if the choice is fueled with emotion and belief.

8.   Emotions that fuel manifestation are love, joy, peace, happiness, goodness, and other positive emotions.

9.   When each idea is transformed into a intention, then each intention may be transformed into a plan, vision, and mission. Then it is chosen as a prime objective for the individual

10.   When the plan is primus it becomes a purpose which is backed by belief.

11.   When firm belief, earnestness and constructive emotion are in back of a purpose, it is energized.

12.   Our belief system must be based on the constant and creative possibility of optimal results and prosperity.   Everyone who is living upright in a spiritual way is deserving and capable of tapping into this abundance.

13.   We become best at co-creating our destiny when we are in spiritual unity with the universe where a person develops the realization of the Divine Presence within one's own self.

14.   We operate most effectively when we are awakened and clear in mind. Attunement and forgiveness of ourselves and others allows us to be free of anger and to live in the present moment fully in an awakened state of mind.

15.   Acceptance - We must believe that prosperity and well-being is our birthright.

16.   Believe that you have wealth and freedom and that you are the essence of creative ability.

17.   Everything that is needed is continually provided by an ever expanding world and universe that is abundant and impersonal.

18.   We must understand the essence or rationale behind the purpose of each desire that we want to cultivate.

19.   Further, we must comprehend in some way how our big ideas will help others along with ourselves to convey the sincere impression of value, worth, and increase.

20.   Before implementing each plan or taking any big step, we evaluate our mental effectiveness. Getting clear and going thought a catharsis of mind. This means to look at your track record, atone, prune, purge, and clear away the mental debris. Begin to use "what works" and start to utilize the best practices which make you efficient.

21.   Clear Objectives - Set specific goals, research and refine them. After the purpose, task and objective is clear, then push forward with persistence.

22.   Results Driven.   What is the mission, destination, vision. Develop affirmations that correlate to the most favorable end-result.

23.   Think, feel and act "AS IF" you are already in possession of the life that you want. Cultivate your emotions and your character around the "As If". You must become what you want which means you become the person who owns the life you desire.

24.   Look at where you are, where you are going and periodically reset the course and navigation to optimize the journey.

25.   Learn to think and speak in a prosperous way that conveys peace, abundance, and increase. Mold the habits and tendencies of your thought. Refuse to accept lack and fear.

26.   Take action. Keep lists and do three things toward your dreams per day, do them constructively to the best of your ability.

27.   Study your life, reflect on your day, decide how to continually improve yourself. Do your homework and do all you can to learn and know your purpose, objectives and master your skills. Be the best at what you do and BE Known for your excellence.

28.   Meditations and Prayer - Write out affirmative meditations such as, "Each day I am improving". Write out 10 statements that are affirming and positive. Contemplate over them each day. You can write out generalized affirmations or very specific ones.

29.   Use the affirmative statements or contemplation, to increase acceptance of our potential and boost our awareness.

30.   Visualize - See yourself in optimal circumstances in your mind's eye and Feel it. If you can visualize the optimal result, then see the next step. Example. See yourself a few pounds leaner toward your optimal weight.

31.   Choose your environment. Select what to feed yourself. Mold your circumstances by your actions and specific thought.

32.   Organize your affairs. Gain the habit of finishing things well. Become excellence, simplify your life, empty the clutter, and redefine your focus. Develop prosperity based routines.

33.   Imprint and affirm your ideals and dreams into your consciousness. The plan, desired thing, or result must be written and then verbalized. It should be claimed into this world using the spoken word.

34.   Make wealth and excellence a priority. Align your thoughts to attract excellence and wealth. Be aware, be open, learn to receive from others, offer praise, and appreciate life. Accept your potentiality, gifts, and abundance.

35.   Circulate your GOOD. Service and Giving - Donate time or money to people or organizations who are the source of your spiritual sustenance.

36.   Sixth Sense - Learn and practice creativity, awareness, and contemplation. Keep a journal, write out ideas, develop and allow a universal flow of inspiration and ideas into your life.

37.   Review and remember your actions. Reflect on what you have done well each day and things you may not have excelled upon. Be determined to be better and do the right thing. Over 200 years ago, Ben Franklin worked his precepts of order each evening. He wanted to be excellent and build his character even at a mature age.

38.   Research ideas - What are your passions, how do your ideas serve? Listen to your intuition & cultivate strategy. Look at what it would take to implement or be successful with your new ideas: then act on them, implement the plan, review the plan and then improve it.

39.   List out streams of income and potential ways to serve and be prosperous. List how you will expand your life. Go past your comfort zones. List goals beyond your expectations and have deadlines of specificity. You can always change the date.

40.   Review your lists and projects. Check off your accomplishments.

41.   Meet with partners, family and/or spouse to define goals.

42.   Discover your natural expression. What is your labor of love. Where do your passions lie. Remember that you work to pay bills, but you should always follow your dreams. Devote 20 percent of your waking hours each week to your passion. If you become great at it, odds are you can earn a living doing it too.

43.   Character - How do you want to BE.? Self respect and self regard can be developed and nurtured. When you rebuild yourself, you will in-turn love yourself better which allows you to be kinder, more generous, and more loving to others.

44.   With Character comes responsibility toward your mental, physical and spiritual health. Do what works to take care of yourself with: diet, exercise, learning, sleep, study, and fellowship.

45.   Associate with those who can help you where you can also help them. Create a network of business and spiritual friends.

46.   Be good to your self. Learn health self regard and cultivate a loving relationship with the Source.

47.   Teaching others - Giving it away to keep it.

48.   Law of Increase and Charisma - Radiate abundance, cheer and enthusiasm. Be contagious with love, cheer, and enthusiasm.

To Manifest Your Potential – Consider These Philosophical Steps

1. What are your desires? Define them.
2. Are you willing to write out what you want to be and what you want for yourself? Can you be specific? Can you ask for more than you ever believed you could achieve?
3. Can you envision achieving them? Try and see them vividly.
4. Do you have the ability to select a definite goal and purpose to complete? Can you specify what you desire in concrete forms on paper and in the spoken word?
5. Are you willing to engage a harmonious relationship with the world and universe? Can you be thankful on a daily basis?
6. Are you willing to take action? Can you begin your dream? Are you willing to ask others for insight, cooperation and help?
7. Are you willing to focus and concentrate on constructive ideals and goals? Can you give your attention to one primary aspiration all day every day? Can you give your all – day in and day out to your ideal or goal?
8. Can you affirm to yourself verbally and with mental images the successful completion of your desires?
9. Are you willing to consider yourself worthy of having a full and rich life. Can you arrange your affairs so that you can receive what you earn or gifts of grace and prosperity.
10. Is it possible for you to believe that you have possession of your desires NOW and IN THIS MOMENT as if you actually HAVE them? Can you imagine yourself owning, being, or having what you really want. Why not?
11. Can you live, speak and act in a constructive way in which your words, thoughts and actions are in concordance with prosperity, abundance, and peace.
12. Are you willing to be grateful for the things you have and the things you do not have yet?
13. Are you willing to engage your desires and passions with emotions of love and gratitude?
14. Can you practice seeing what you want in your mind's eye on a regular basis?

NOTES

✓

✓

✓

✓

✓

✓

✓

✓

✓

AUTOR BIO – GEORGE S MENTZ, ESQ.

Commissioner George Mentz JD MBA CILS is a global
entrepreneur trained in international law who has worked
or traveled in over 40 nations worldwide. Mentz is an
international award winning success author, multiple
award winning professor, and educator based in the

United States. Mentz was ranked #2 in the world as an influencer in the area of wealth management in 2020.

Mentz is the first law professor with a Doctor of Jurisprudence in the USA to be multi credentialed in: international law, management consulting, wealth management/financial consulting, and financial planning along with having an earned MBA and JD degree and US law license.

Counselor Mentz is one of the few JD/MBA holders in the USA to earn a CILS Graduate Cert./Diploma in International Legal Studies. Mentz is the Titular Seigneur of the Feif of Blondel in Guernsey which is a legally registered Fief that is over 700 years old.

Mentz was appointed as a US Commissioner for the White House Presidential Scholars Program in the USA after volunteering for Bush, Obama and Trump. Mentz received his DSS Doctor of Spiritual Studies from the Emerson Institute and is a Licensed Member of the ANTN Affiliated New Thought Network.

Bibliography:
Black Elk, N. and Neihardt, J. G. (2000) Black Elk Speaks, Lincoln: University of Nebraska Press.

Capra, F. (1989) The Tao of Physics: An Exploration of the Parallels between Modern Physics and Eastern Mysticism, London: Flamingo

Cleary, T. (1992) The Essential Tao: An Initiation in the Heart of Taoism through the Authentic Tao Te Ching and the Inner Teachings of ChuangTzu, New Jersey: Castle Books.

Collier, R. (1999) The Secret of the Ages, Oak Harbor, WA: Robert Collier Publications

Covey, S. R. (1989) The 7 Habits of Highly Effective People, London: Simon & Schuster.

Drury, Nevill. The Elements of Shamanism. Rockport, Mass.: Element Books, 1989. Eason, Cassandra. The Handbook of Ancient Wisdom. New York: Sterling Publishing, 1997.

Muhammad Al-Ghazzali (1909) The Alchemy of Happiness, trans. Claud Field, London: J. Murray; also at www.sacred-texts.com.

Goleman, D. (1998) Working with Emotional Intelligence, London: Bloomsbury.

Goodwin, Joscelyn. Mystery Religions In The Ancient World. San Francisco: Harper and Row, 1981

Grimm, Jacob. Teutonic Mythology. 4 vols. New York: Dover, 1966.

Franklin, B. (1993) "The Way to Wealth" in Benjamin Franklin: Autobiography and Other Writings, O. Seavey (ed.), Oxford: Oxford University Press.

Heisler, Roger. Path To Power, It's All In Your Mind. York Beach, Maine: Samuel Weiser, 1990

Heschel, A. J. (1975) The Sabbath: Its Meaning for Modern Man, New York: Farrar, Straus and Giroux.

Hill, N. & Stone, W. C. (1990) Success through a Positive Mental Attitude, London: Thorsons.

Hill, N. (1960) Think and Grow Rich, New York: Fawcett Crest.

Hollander, Lee M., trans. The Poetic Edda. 2d ed. Austin: University of Texas Press, 1962.

Jones, Gwyn. A History ofthe Vikings. London: OxfordUniversity Press, 1973

Jung, C. G. (1978) Memories, Dreams, Reflections, Glasgow: William Collins. The Book of Margery Kempe (1936) trans. W. Butler-Bowdon, London: Jonathan Cape.

Krishnamurti, J. (1970) Think on These Things, New York: Harper & Row.

MacGregor-Mathers, S. L., trans. The Book of the Sacred Magic of Abra-Melin the Mage. Chicago: de Laurence, 1932.

Meyer, Marvin W. The Ancient Mysteries: A Source Book. San Francisco: Harper and Row, 1987

O'Donohue, J. (1998) Anam Cara: Spiritual Wisdom from the Celtic World, London: Bantam.

Pirsig, R. M. (1999) Zen and the Art of Motorcycle Maintenance, London: Vintage.

Redfield, J. (1993) The Celestine Prophecy: An Adventure, New York: Bantam.

Schucman, H. & Thetford, W. (1996) A Course in Miracles, New York: Viking

Scovel Shinn, F. (1978) The Secret Door to Success, Camarillo, CA: De Vorss & Co.

Storms, G. Anglo-Saxon Magic. The Hague: Nijhoff, 1948.

Sun Tzu (2002) The Art of War, Denma Translation Group, Boston: Shambhala.

Suzuki, S. (2003) Zen Mind, Beginner's Mind: Informal Talks on Zen Meditation and Practice, New York: Weatherhill, Inc.

Swedenborg, E. (1976) Heaven and Hell, trans. George F. Dole, New York: Swedenborg Foundation.

Teresa of Avila (1989) Interior Castle, New York: Doubleday.

Tolle, E. (2001) The Power of Now: A Guide to Spiritual Enlightenment, Sydney: Hodder.

Tracy, B. (1993) Maximum Achievement: Strategies and Skills that Will Unlock Your Hidden Powers to Succeed, New York: Fireside.

Turville-Petre, E. O. G. Myth and Religion of the North. New York: Holt, Rinehart and Winston, 1964.

Warren, R. (2002) The Purpose-Driven Life, Grand Rapids: Zondervan.

Wiseman, R. (2003) The Luck Factor: Change Your Luck—And Change Your Life, London: Century.

Ziglar, Z. (2000) See You at the Top: 25th Anniversary Edition, Gretna, LA: Pelican Publishing.

---

[i] https://www.tonyrobbins.com/health-vitality/biohacking-for-beginners/
[ii] Pg. 160 The American Journal of Sociology, Volume 72 Albion Woodbury Small, Ellsworth Faris, Ernest Watson Burgess University of Chicago Press, 1895 - Social sciences
[iii] Architectural Record - Volume 155 - Page 65 - McGraw-Hill, 1891 - Architecture
https://books.google.com › books